An OPUS book

Democracy at Work

OPUS General Editors

Keith Thomas
Alan Ryan
Peter Medawar

Tom Schuller

Democracy at Work

Oxford New York

OXFORD UNIVERSITY PRESS

1985

Oxford University Press, Walton Street, Oxford OX2 6DP
Oxford New York Toronto
Delhi Bombay Calcutta Madras Karachi
Kuala Lumpur Singapore Hong Kong Tokyo
Nairobi Dar es Salaam Cape Town
Melbourne Auckland
and associated companies in
Beirut Berlin Ibadan Nicosia

Oxford is a trade mark of Oxford University Press

© Tom Schuller 1985

First published 1985 as an Oxford University Press paperback
and simultaneously in a hardback edition

British Library Cataloguing in Publication Data
Schuller, Tom
Democracy at work.—(OPUS)
1. Management—Employee participation
I. Title II. Series
331'.01'12 HD5650
ISBN 0-19-219186-1
ISBN 0-19-289168-5 Pbk

Library of Congress Cataloging in Publication Data
Schuller, Tom.
Democracy at work.
(OPUS)
Bibliography: p. Includes index.
1. Industrial management—Employee participation.
2. Industrial relations. I. Title. II. Series.
HD5650.S396 1985 331'.01'12 85-8780
ISBN 0-19-219186-1
ISBN 0-19-289168-5 (pbk.)

Set by Colset Private Ltd.
Printed in Great Britain by
Biddles Ltd., Guildford

Acknowledgements

Thanks are due first to Eithne Johnstone, without whose unfailing helpfulness and skill the book would never have emerged; to Colin Crouch, Freda Edis, Laurie Hunter, and Alan Ryan for useful comments on earlier drafts; and to the members of my family for their continued support.

Contents

Abbreviations

ACAS	Advisory, Conciliation, and Arbitration Service
AFL–CIO	American Federation of Labor and Congress of Industrial Organizations
ASLEF	Associated Society of Locomotive Engineers and Firemen
AUEW	Amalgamated Union of Engineering Workers
BSC	British Steel Corporation
CBI	Confederation of British Industry
CFDT	Confédération Française Democratique du Travail
CGT	Confédération Generale du Travail
EEF	Engineering Employers' Federation
IPM	Institute of Personnel Management
LO	Landsorganisationen (Sweden)
MSC	Manpower Services Commission
NALGO	National and Local Government Officers' Association
NEDC	National Economic Development Council
NUPE	National Union of Public Employees
NUR	National Union of Railwaymen
OECD	Organization for Economic Co-operation and Development
SAIMA	Shipbuilding and Allied Industries Management Association
TSSA	Transport Salaried Staffs' Association
TGWU	Transport and General Workers' Union
TUC	Trades Union Congress

Introduction

There are some subjects on which judgements and analyses first presented years ago can be dusted off and resubmitted as plausible contributions to the current debate. Democracy at work is one such subject.[1]

> While as a citizen he [the thinking workman] has an equal share in determining the most momentous issues, about which he may know very little, his opinion is seldom asked or considered, and he has practically no voice in determining the conditions of his daily life, except in so far as trade-union action has secured it. Indeed, where management is inefficient and autocratic he is frequently compelled to watch waste and mistakes of which he is perfectly well aware without any right of intervention whatever. And this, despite the fact that when these errors issue in diminished business for the firm concerned, he, and not the management, will be the first to suffer by short-time working or complete loss of employment.[2]

Correct the sexist tone and the rather ingenuous view of citizen power, and the comment of over fifty years ago would find its place easily in modern discourse. From very varying political perspectives similar points have been made repeatedly: the contrast between political rights and rights at work, the waste of knowledge and talent, the unaccountability of decision-makers, and so on.

The persistence of such themes gives an impression (not wholly false) of repetition and sameness. But of course the difference is not just that early terminology is antiquated; the terms themselves have different points of reference and reflect different values and aspirations. We still have the notion of autocracy, but it may be used to refer to behaviour which some decades ago would have been regarded as perfectly normal practice. One decade's shop-floor insolence is the next's relaxed industrial relations.

Expectations and standards rise, repeatedly defying society to declare an issue solved. This is entirely healthy—indeed, the physical healthiness of the work environment provides an example. Some hazards are both new and particularly obnoxious, but in general it would be fair to compare average physical working conditions favourably with those of a hundred years ago. Yet quite rightly there

is a continuing concern both to upgrade the conditions themselves
and to raise the standards used for judging health and safety. The
number of deaths at work may have declined, but the level of industrial mortality—and morbidity—is still unacceptable. The problem
remains, demanding regular and urgent restatement.

We need, then, in addition to an awareness of the persistence of
many of the issues, an appreciation of flux and change, in order both
to understand the present and to avoid conservative immobilism.
The pattern of authority at work has demonstrably changed: new
institutions have been developed and new practices recognized
whereby working people can participate in decisions affecting them.
On the other hand, the constant motion has not been all in one
direction. Progress is diverted or stunted by combinations of economic, political, and social circumstances, with no unambiguous
current in favour of participation. Judgements about the direction
reflect value positions held in respect of the interests of individuals,
groups, or classes, and in respect of the power relationships which
obtain between them. People's judgements of a trade union, for
example, will reflect the degree to which they are factually informed
about its history, membership, and role, their view on the appro-
priateness of its members' current position within industrial society,
and their outlook on more general matters such as the balance
between labour and capital. Similarly their judgements of an individual's right to participate at the workplace will depend on a mixture
of more or less factual knowledge about the nature of the work and
workers' competences, and more or less subjective assessments of
what constitutes an acceptable distribution of power.

As I explain in Chapter 2, I see conflict as an inherent if uneven
feature of society. Some conflicts derive directly from the character
of capitalist society (understood as the domination of production
processes by private ownership and the market); others are more
plausibly attributed to a range of factors more or less independent of
the form of ownership. To aspire to rid society altogether of conflict
seems to me Utopian, and to seek to explain it in terms of dichotomies
alone, unnecessarily constrictive. Conflict stems from multiple
sources, generated with very varying degrees of force, and this is
reflected in the process of decision-making at work as it is in the wider
society. Power-sharing at work will not dissolve tensions, though it
may play some part in avoiding or reducing clashes which benefit
none of the parties involved. Nor is it necessarily the case that greater
democracy inspires greater efficiency, whether that is defined by
physical output or other, less crude, indices. On the other hand it is

inconceivable that current patterns of authority and power will—or should—remain as they are. Individually and collectively, people will continue to seek to strengthen some interests and weaken others. Their motives are diverse and not always narrowly self-centred.

This book's basic premise is that we should be actively exploring ways of achieving a more equitable distribution of power at the workplace, but it does not engage directly with the broader currents of political discourse. It contains no concise summaries of relevant theoretical approaches and few descriptive accounts of participation initiatives or systems.[3] Its aim is modest: to provide a relatively straightforward way of looking both at the general theme of worker participation and at specific issues which have contemporary significance, emphasizing meanwhile that the contours of the debate are undergoing constant change.

Participation: the moving target

Let us get the definitional task over with. There is a whole cluster of terms—employee participation, joint decision-making, employee involvement, industrial democracy, workers' control, self-management—which suggest a degree of employee influence at work. They make up a close but often internally competitive family. They are not synonymous—some clearly imply a more radical redistribution of power than others—but neither can they be easily ranked in some smooth progression. Their respective currency varies according to the political and cultural context. In the UK the term 'industrial democracy' predominated in the last decade, sanctioned by its inclusion in the remit of an official Committee of Inquiry (the Bullock Committee). But as two active proponents of democratization observed in the mid-1970s, industrial democracy is a term which is 'so general, all-embracing and has such wide appeal that politicians and philosophers of all shades of opinion prefer to pay lip-service to it, rather than to oppose it outright'.[4] In the first half of the 1980s, the political climate has sharpened sufficiently for Conservative politicians to reject industrial democracy as an ideologically unacceptable incursion into the rights of capital, and to seek to redefine the issue in terms of 'employee involvement' and 'communication'.[5] Nevertheless there is still a far greater verbal consensus over the need for some kind of participation in decision-making than there is practical agreement over form and substance.

We cannot, like Humpty-Dumpty, use words to mean what we want them to mean. On the contrary, we need to examine critically the claims that are made for initiatives which purport to embody greater democracy, and compare promise with reality. Research repeatedly shows how participants have divergent conceptions of what is involved in a particular initiative; some are contented with the outcome but cannot understand others' expressions of frustration or disappointment. The problem for any definition of a live social phenomenon is to capture the sense of motion and change. In some ways it is like shooting at the ducks which bobble across a fairground stall. It is hard enough to hit the target; even then, the duck re-emerges upright some seconds later. Moreover, tomorrow the whole stall will have moved, as the fair travels on to its next pitch. The dynamic of worker participation is far less repetitive, and its successive outcomes far less predictable. Shifts in the structure of the world economy, in the nature of modern capitalism, in the character and above all the aspirations of people inside and outside the workplace—these all make it unwise even to attempt to pin down the concept definitively.

I shall therefore opt for a banal but flexible statement of the theme: democracy at work refers to the participation by working people in the decision-making processes which govern their working lives. The participation may be formal or informal, direct or indirect; it may cover one, some, or all of the areas of decision-making. 'Democratization' refers to the enhancement of participation. This may be uneven, patchy, and temporary; moreover, what is for one group a significant step forward is for others unimportant, or a goal they have already achieved. That said, I shall use 'participation' and 'industrial democracy' almost interchangeably.

The swirl and the different contexts of workplace relations make it impossible to propose a single conceptual framework to fit all cases of participation. Any comprehensive review of the various typologies would send abstract terms ricocheting around at all angles, like a fiercely contested conceptual squash match. But a review of a small number of such schemata will give the reader a fair idea of the different angles from which the subject can be viewed and mapped out.

The extension of collective bargaining

The majority of decisions are taken at their workplace by union and management representatives carrying out their daily unspectacular business—in other words, they are a matter of bread-and-butter industrial relations. Orthodox collective bargaining is in one sense the dominant mode for employees to participate in decisions, through their union representatives. The spread and extension of collective bargaining is therefore an integral part of the democratization of work. For some, indeed, industrial democracy is to be interpreted solely in terms of the extension of collective bargaining and there is no need to contemplate any other forms. There are three interrelated dimensions along which bargaining is being extended: substantive areas, organizational levels, and timing.

Areas

Over the past two decades, negotiations have come to cover areas which were previously the sole prerogative of management. They have shifted several of the 'frontiers of control'.[6] Fringe benefits such as holidays, sick-leave, and pensions are subject more and more to joint regulation. 'Pay and conditions' evolve into 'the total remuneration package'. Joint agreements governing the conditions under which new technology may be introduced are now widely canvassed, though the actual extent of their remit can be questioned. Not everything is open to negotiation—strategic financial decisions, for example, are still well outside the collective bargaining arena. But the potential for extending the process is at least recognized in principle in trade union quarters, and by some managements.

Organizational levels

For some time the general trend in the private sector has been a decentralization of bargaining, with responsibilities devolved down to local level. However, a substantial survey of industrial relations published in 1984 suggests that the focus of bargaining is shifting from plant to company level,[7] and the dominant organizational tendency within industry has been growth by conglomeration, with major decisions often further removed from the actual place of production. Just as labour has become aware of the need to extend negotiations into new areas, so it has been forced to realize that this cannot be effective without recognition of bargaining rights at new levels of corporate decision-making. Involvement in strategic decisions may mean moving some functions away from localized bargaining and seeking the centre, however difficult that may be even to locate.

Timing

Most decisions at work are still taken unilaterally by management. Only then does the work-force react, with differing degrees of compliance. Obviously there are occasions when unions take the initiative, for instance in presenting the annual wage claim. But in most cases— even in the areas which we have specifically mentioned above—their participation is passive or reactive: tolerating routine or objecting to change. The third dimension of extended collective bargaining is for unions to seek to influence decisions earlier in the process of their formulation, or even to originate them entirely themselves. Instead of accepting that management come forward with proposals to which they are to react, they produce the proposals themselves. In this way, involvement delves further back. It can also extend further forwards, into decisions with long-term implications whose effects will only be seen some considerable time in the future.

All three dimensions are illustrated by the initiative of the Lucas Aerospace workers. Concerned both for their own jobs and to use their skills for other than military ends, they put forward a package of proposals for alternative products which they argued would be both commercially viable and socially valuable. The plan was produced by a Combine Committee, drawn from different plants within the company. The workers' plan thus represents an attempt by a work-force to influence the strategy of the company, extending the bargaining process into new areas such as research and product development, and pitching it at corporate level. And although one of the impulses behind it was to ward off threats to jobs—these were already perceived in the early 1970s—it represented an initiative as well as a response, raising issues which extend well into the future.[8]

There are several reasons why the Lucas initiative cannot be regarded as typical: the highly skilled nature of the prime movers, unusually charismatic leadership and dynamic exploitation of public relations. Even with these advantages the plan has not achieved implementation, and its high political profile has made a cool assessment of its strengths and weaknesses more difficult. The question of who is to decide what is a 'socially useful' product, and according to what criteria, remains unsolved. Conceptually, however, it has shown how unstable the frontiers of control are.

Beyond, besides, and between bargaining: dimensions of participation

Theorists are paid to worry about categories; other people manage without them. The boundaries between negotiation and other modes of participation resemble the purview of a drunk. At any given moment the picture is not clearly defined; even when it is, the next moment it has somehow changed its contours. Rather than attempt a typology of institutions (consultative committees, works councils, worker representation at board levels and so on), I shall deal with decision-making as a process, and with accounts which set out ways of classifying how far that process is a democratic one. 'Decision-making' itself has limitations as a basic descriptive term; it disguises the routine and implicit way in which power is commonly exercised, and imputes a greater degree of conscious rationality to the process than is often the case.

A general political science approach is given by Carole Pateman in her book *Participation and Democratic Theory*. She begins by observing:

The whole point about industrial participation is that it involves a modification, to a greater or less degree, of the orthodox authority structure; namely one where decision making is the 'prerogative' of management, in which workers play no part. This is what is overlooked by many writers on management . . . Participation may, as we have seen, be effective in increasing efficiency, but what is important is that these writers use the term 'participation' to refer not just to a method of decision making, but also to cover techniques used to persuade employees to accept decisions that have *already* been made by the management. Situations of this type, where no participation in decision making in fact takes place, we shall . . . call pseudo participation.[9]

Pateman then moves on to participation itself, which she analyses along two basic dimensions. She distinguishes between full and partial *degrees* of participation. The key distinction here is who is in a position to make the final decision. 'Partial' participation exists when workers can only influence the decision without having equal power to decide the outcome. 'Because they are "workers" they are in the (unequal) position of permanent subordinates; the final "prerogative" of decision making rests with the permanent superiors, with management.'[10] 'Full' participation, on the other hand, occurs when each individual member of a decision-making body has equal power to determine the outcome of decisions, for instance about the allocation of work.

Pateman's second distinction is between *levels* of participation. She restricts herself to two: low and high. The former 'refers broadly to those management decisions relating to control of day-to-day shop activity, while the higher level refers to decisions that relate to the running of the whole enterprise, decisions on investment, marketing and so forth'.[11] Most writers agree on the analytical need to distinguish between different levels of decision-making, and some follow this dual distinction, even if they use different terminology—corporate and job-related, or strategic and employee-related are just two examples. Others, however, find it too coarse for their purposes. Wall and Lischeron identify three levels.[12] *Local* participation occurs at the lowest levels in the organizational hierarchy, and concerns decisions immediately relevant to the workers themselves and characteristically made by workers themselves, their supervisors, or jointly. Examples of local participation are the scheduling of tasks and the allocation of duties amongst available workers. *Medium* participation refers to the activities 'which traditionally fall within the authority of middle managers'. These tend to affect large numbers of workers, typically a whole department, and include recruitment, promotion, and training policies. Finally, *distant* participation relates to the highest reaches of an organizational hierarchy, and the involvement of workers in decisions determining the growth of the organization and its major financial activities.

Clearly they have simply cut the cake differently. One could suggest still finer gradings, and it is certainly important to see how far there is variation between organizations in the levels at which similar decisions are reached. One of the recurrent arguments against greater democratization is that there is only one optimal way of organizing affairs, to be decided upon by technical experts. The greater the variety demonstrated in the allocation of decisions to different levels (without directly corresponding success and failure rates), the less plausible this argument is.

Talk of cakes and levels conjures up an image of tiers of sponge, jam, and cream, neatly layered but blending nicely together. Yet the levels may very well not combine smoothly but grate against each other. Participants at one level are constrained and frustrated by decisions taken at another level at which they have no influence. Even 'rational' decision-making is not necessarily a smooth process. Awkward and perhaps unsatisfactory trade-offs will continue to confront those involved, within democratic structures no less than any other.

The levels referred to are internal to the organization. It will already be clear that discussions of industrial democracy tend to focus on the organization, or on a unit within it (plant, branch, etc.), and I shall generally conform to this pattern. However, as the next section makes clear, organizational decision-making is shaped to a significant extent by external considerations such as the macro-economic climate. There is therefore scope for participation at levels of decision-making above the organizational. Most obviously at national level there are modes of participation which have been characterized as 'corporatist'; typically they involve representatives of central confederations of capital and labour conferring with the government on issues which, it is thought, cannot be left to decision-makers at a lower level. The concept of corporatism is a fertile source of conceptual dispute, even as to its validity;[13] what cannot be denied is the interrelationship between power and participation at (sub)organizational and supraorganizational levels.

Wall and Lischeron also introduce a distinction between *forms* of participation:

The primary distinction is between *direct* and *indirect* (or representative) participation. The former includes any or all of the situations in which workers participate personally in decision-making. This they may do individually, or in the context of a group, but the defining characteristic is that they present their own views, they speak for themselves. Indirect participation is representative in nature. It includes any or all of the ways in which workers are represented by others in decision-making processes.[14]

It is sometimes assumed that direct participation is somehow 'better' than indirect. Certainly it is important to assess the extent of democratization, i.e. how far different levels of employee are involved.[15] It is also as well to be aware of the limitations of representative forms of democracy; the installation of representative machinery cannot infuse a body politic with democratic life. But it is the relationship between different forms of participation which is crucial, rather than the absolute degree of the direct form. Roger Garaudy rightly attacks the 'utopian picture . . . of everybody taking decisions about everything all of the time', suggesting instead that the best definition of 'workers' control' is the systematic application of the rule that problems should be solved at the level at which they arise.[16]

The same distinction, between direct and indirect participation, is made by the Industrial Democracy in Europe group, though they sagely observe that 'it is nothing like as transparent as it might appear at first sight'.[17] This group conducted collaborative research into industrial democracy in twelve countries, and the nature of the exercise perhaps accounts for the laboriousness of their typology. They select *scope* and *amount* as the two basic dimensions of participation. The former denotes the number of decision types in which an individual is involved (similar to Pateman's and Wall and Lischeron's distinctions), the latter the extent of the individual's involvement. This brings in its trail a distinction between *de jure* (legally required) and *de facto* (actual) participation. A further classification is established according to the variations in the 'importance' of the decisions in which employees are involved, a line being drawn between *subjective* and *objective* importance. Finally there is some indication that participation by *individuals* and *groups* should be differently approached (though the report shows some ambiguity on this score).

Indigestible though such typologies are in the abstract, this brief review has provided a guide to the way democracy at work has commonly been conceptualized. The degree, level, form, and formality will all vary across workplaces and countries and over time, continuously or sporadically. What is in practice seen as desirable is a matter partly of general political values, and partly of assessing the relationship between democracy and other characteristics of decision-making at work (for example productive efficiency). There is no necessary incompatibility, but on the other hand the obvious fact that different degrees of participation must occur at different levels of decision-making obliges everyone—the most ardent proponents and opponents of democracy alike—to make choices. The specific issues discussed in subsequent chapters should help to clarify what these choices are. But one further piece of definitional discussion is required.

'Industrial' and 'economic' democracy

In the next chapter we shall examine in more detail how adequate the term 'industrial' is to cover working society. I shall argue that it still clothes the torso but that non-industrial limbs and other excrescences protrude at every corner, and that it no longer neatly fits even the trunk itself. But 'industrial democracy' is unsatisfactory for other reasons, which have encouraged the use of 'economic democracy' as a broader and more suitable concept.

Participation at the level of the plant or organization is constrained by broader factors relating to the ownership of capital. This has long been an issue in broad political and economic theory, most obviously in analyses of Western capitalist societies. But with the growth of complex enterprises moving across sectoral and national boundaries, and the consequent removal of decision-making power further and further from the point of production, the limitations of a greater employee influence which is confined to the immediate workplace become more apparent. Lower-level participation finds itself bumping its head against ceilings imposed by conceptions of the rights of private capital. The relationship between control and ownership thus becomes a more prominent issue.

Throughout the industrialized world high levels of unemployment have weakened labour and led to some slackening of the drive for institutional forms of democratization, whether through the extension of collective bargaining or of other modes of participation. On the other hand they have seen the development of various initiatives concerned with new forms of capital distribution. Some moves (Employee Stock-Ownership Plans in the US, profit-sharing in the UK) represent wholly individualized forms of financial participation and it is highly doubtful whether they will have any effect on patterns of control at work. But there are other initiatives which have more substantial implications for the distribution of decision-making power. These include the promotion of co-operatives and the transformation of companies into co-operative form, where the ownership of a single organization is modified in one of a number of possible ways. They also include the most prominent scheme for collective financial participation, the wage-earner funds fathered by Rudolf Meidner. More concretely, there has been substantial growth in employee participation in the management of pension funds, which can constitute vast sums of capital. We examine these empirical and theoretical developments towards economic democracy in Chapters 4 and 5.

Other considerations along these lines are of a more philosophical nature. T. H. Marshall refers to three types of citizenship rights which have emerged (sequentially) in modern times: legal, political, and social (or welfare).[18] Anthony Giddens argues that such rights should not be dismissed as bourgeois freedoms, but also comments that they do not extend to the workplace, where the sale of labour-power remains the 'other face' or the liberal–democratic state.[19] The natural response is to consider what form such rights at work should take. In recent years this has been most actively pursued, in both theoretical and policy terms, in Scandinavia. Social democrat historians have followed Marshall (though starting from his second phase) in identifying successive stages of universal suffrage and welfare rights. When the next step is considered, it is argued that significant changes in the distribution of power at work can be established within a system of private ownership, but these will be constrained by the conflict between the rights of property and the rights of labour. This generates pressure for a thorough overhaul of the relationship between capital and labour:[20] in other words a move to *economic* democracy, which embraces not only the issues customarily addressed under the heading of 'industrial democracy', but also the question of new forms of capital ownership and control.

The idea of economic democracy may or may not 'take' generally. It is not, in any case, a novel concept.[21] We began this chapter by illustrating the durability of certain terms, but labels can change as well as contents. Shelley put it definitively: 'Naught may endure but Mutability.'

Conclusion

The themes discussed in this introduction will recur as I attempt to provide a range of different perspectives on a multi-faceted topic. The aim is to give a sense of democratization as a diverse and uneven process, through a mix of abstract and concrete discussion. Chapter 1 traces out changes in the features of working society, focusing on the composition and organization of its work-force, and the pattern of employment. The changes in the separate features add up to a very different profile to that which presented itself to the Webbs when they gave two-volume support to the topic of industrial democracy at the beginning of the century.[22] Chapter 2 sets out some simple conceptual parameters for the study of power and conflict as they relate to the process of decision-making at work. Chapter 3 has an overtly historical flavour. It considers both the rather ingenuous view of democratization as a smooth evolutionary process and the more cynical judgement that there is a dominant pattern of cyclical repetition, leading nowhere.

Chapter 4 examines individual and collective forms of financial participation and economic democracy. It suggests a framework within which such diverse initiatives as profit-sharing schemes and wage-earner funds can be compared. Chapters 5 and 6 deal with two specific areas of decision-making, pension scheme management and health and safety, which have emerged as significant examples of joint decision-making in recent years. The tension between political and industrial democracy is discussed in Chapter 7 as an issue which can no longer be conveniently relegated to the sidelines. The subject of worker directors is delayed until Chapter 8. This avoids the identification of industrial democracy with board-level representation, but the Bullock proposals for worker directors placed a number of questions on the agenda which have still to be adequately recognized. Chapter 9 looks at the relationship between democratization and the control of occupational and representative skills. The last chapter argues that democracy at work necessarily involves the articulation of collective interests. It sketches three dimensions along which these can be defined, illustrating them by recapitulating on themes discussed earlier.

1 The changing profile of work

I have just pulled off my shelves five books to do with working life. The oldest, *The New Unionism* (1974), by Ken Coates and Tony Topham, has on its cover a heavy black spanner, firmly gripped by two muscular and indubitably male hands. Ben Hooberman's *An Introduction to British Trade Unions* (published in the same year) carries a similar motif: a clenched fist, a detail from a banner belonging to the Electrical Trades' Union (founded 1890). The cover of Colin Crouch's *Politics of Industrial Relations* (1979) shows an Indian wrestling match between a hirsute forearm sticking out from a rolled-up blue sleeve on one side and a pin-striped and cuffed arm on the other.

The other two books date from 1981. Tony Eccles's account of a workers' co-operative, *Under New Management*, has six figures on the front, all male. One, greying, middle-aged, and distinguished-looking, wears an elegant three-piece suit and a buttonhole, one a sports jacket and tie. The other figure with a tie wears a white, scientific-looking overall. At one side is a painter in dungarees, at the other a besweatered figure in boots with a hammer sticking out of his jeans pocket. Sitting in the middle is a bearded man with an apron. Stephen Hill's *Competition and Control at Work* eschews such detail. It has nine silhouette figures, one recognizably female. Another sits at a draughtsman's or designer's desk (judging from the anglepoise lamp and high stool) and a third peers through a microscope. The rest are indescribably occupied —except that the two middle figures have their hands firmly plunged in their pockets, perhaps representing the un- or under-employed.

The point of such an unstructured excursion into iconography is simply to remind us how stereotypes exist, but also how they can change. If we are setting out to get a clearer picture of democracy at work, we must begin with some understanding of what work is, and what directions it is taking.

How far does one era's experience of work differ from another's? Probably the biggest single divide between the decade up until 1985 and the rest of the post-war period is the growth of joblessness. Even those who have not been themselves directly affected by the threat or reality of unemployment have had their perceptions of work shaped by the knowledge of the labour market conditions which surround them. For those in secure positions, the problem of being actually without work may not arise, but career avenues are blocked off and professional development stunted by the same events which cause others to lose their jobs or fail altogether to gain a foothold in the labour market. It is possible that members of their families—especially younger ones—will at least have experienced major difficulties in finding work. It is a small and diminishing band whose attitudes to work will have been left untouched.

We shall return later to the question of unemployment, especially in considering the relative strengths of the different parties involved in decision-making. For the moment, however, we are concerned with those in work: who are they, what kinds of work do they have, and what are the ties between them and their representatives? The central theme will be how far we have moved from the idea of the typical employee as a male, manual worker in a privately owned single-plant manufacturing unit. Having traced out the changes in the work-force, we can cover, with similar brevity, significant modifications in organizational structures, including that of collective bargaining.

However, the question 'what is work?' cannot be answered by looking only at changes in the distribution of formal employment, on the assumption that the boundary between work and non-work is sharply defined. Even in legal terms the position is far from clear-cut. In a recent Inland Revenue case (*Clear* v. *Smith* (1981)) the judge said:

It cannot be doubted, in my judgement, that if the defendant had been carrying out this activity for reward that activity would have been work. The word 'work' has to be given its ordinary meaning in this context and it would be satisfied by showing that the defendant with his car and trailer was carrying scrap if the scrap had been carried for remuneration.

The whole question here on the first argument in this case is whether it makes any difference that the work should be done not for remuneration but done in the manner which I have described. I think this is above all a point for the justices as a question of fact and degree. One cannot lay down as a general proposition that an unpaid activity is not work. As was suggested in argument, no housewife would be ready to accept that proposition with equanimity. On the other hand it does not follow that every activity which is backed up by remuneration is work. It is a question of fact and degree for the justices to give the word a common-sense meaning in its context as part of a declaration.

The judge's pronouncement refers to two issues which make it important to avoid the identification of work with waged employment.

First is the role of *domestic labour* and the growing recognition that great numbers of women provide services without which the formal economy could not function and for which they mostly receive payment only on a discretionary basis or in kind—in the form of housekeeping money and through access to goods and property purchased with the husband's wages. Those concerned with sexual equality disagree about whether domestic labour should be formally rewarded. Some see it as a necessary way of achieving recognition for the multi-skilled job of cleaner, cook, child-rearer, social hostess, and so on, others as a misguided proposal which would tie women more firmly to the house. In either case it is important to recognize the two-way relationship between the home and the workplace. The current production system shapes the sexual division of labour and domestic structures. It pushes women into lower-paid jobs with few career prospects, or into staying at home altogether. At the same time, pressure is put on the family to divide its own roles and responsibilities to suit the requirements of employment. Although there is no simple correspondence, workers' experience of the way authority is exercised at work seeps into their behaviour at home. The converse is also true, though perhaps to a lesser extent. Family life affects the attitudes of workers to their employment in diverse ways. Greater equality between the sexes domestically can have a number of effects, often contradictory. It may make men more sensitive to discriminatory practices at work and less inclined to accept hierarchy, but at the same time new domestic obligations may reduce their willingness to commit themselves to union work, previously made possible by female domestic labour.[1]

The promotion of domestic labour as a salient issue has its origins mainly in the social and political drive to combat discrimination. It has been reinforced by the parallel development, caused more by faltering economic growth, of the so-called *informal economy*. Voluntarily or not, increasing numbers of people are earning a living outside formal employment, with varying degrees of legality. A part-time wage may be supplemented by unofficial economic activity on the side, or a household may be wholly dependent on its own resources for its income. Bartering, casual work, 'homers', enterprise, fiddling—the activities which, like domestic labour, do not show up on the official employment statistics (nor add to official GNP) but which represent a significant part of many people's lives and incomes. Almost by definition, due to its unofficial nature, the size and character of the informal economy is hard to map out, but in a time of high unemployment it can only be increasing.[2]

Ideological recognition of domestic labour combined with the growth of the informal economy may mean that the relationship between the home and the workplace will be taken more seriously than before. With the added complication of children's rights the prospect of the democratization of the domestic workplace raises some intriguing issues. Certainly we shall have to look more closely at the interaction between formal work and other activities. But I turn now to more familiar contours of the labour map, to see how they are being redrawn and to comment briefly on their relevance to democracy at work.

Work-force profile

When, in the famous Labour party debate over nationalization in 1959, Hugh Gaitskell referred to the democratization of work, he confined himself to agriculture and manufacturing, as if these were the only significant sectors in which people worked. Today the numbers employed in agriculture are very small, especially in the UK. Their rights as employees are debated mainly in relation to tied cottages, rather than their say in farmyard decision-making. (The work-force is, almost by definition, geographically dispersed and difficult to organize. It is hard, therefore, to see pressure building up for greater democracy in this sector.)

Table 1   Civilian employment by sector in selected OECD countries 1968–1981 (1975 = 100)

	1968			1981		
	Agriculture	Industry	Other	Agriculture	Industry	Other
Austria	137.4	97.3	84.9	81.9	98.3	110.5
France	150.1	96.8	83.2	85.3	92.1	111.2
Japan	149.5	92.3	85.0	84.3	105.2	113.6
Netherlands	117.9	110.0	89.2	93.5	91.7	115.7
Sweden	130.3	103.8	80.2	90.8	89.3	114.9
UK	126.0	110.1	89.6	92.9	84.7	105.0
US	111.4	102.3	80.5	100.3	114.8	119.0
OECD total	124.1	98.5	83.7	90.3	101.5	114.4

Source: OECD, *Labour Force Statistics 1970–1981* (1983).

Table 1 shows the global shift that has taken place in the distribution of the work-force between different *employment sectors* over the last fifteen years. Table 2 gives the current position for the UK. It underlines how dominant the service sector has become, with over twice as many employees as manufacturing industry; it also illustrates the association of this trend with the growth of female employment.

Table 2   UK Employment, 1984 (000)

	Male	Female	Total
Agriculture, forestry, fishing	214	92	366
Manufacturing, production, and construction	4,529	1,667	6,196
Services	6,117	7,164	13,281

Source: Employment Gazette 92:12 (Dec. 1984).

There are two notes of caution to be sounded. First, the changes have not been a series of smooth transitions, from agriculture to industry to services. Many individuals are drowned in the crossing from one category to another as the process of industrial change destroys their established occupation, and the picture cannot be one of a population safely wading up the beaches of the service sector. Secondly, there are fundamental weaknesses in the overall categorization of employment. At a basic level there are two very different types of classification:

The first is employment as classified by industrial sector, so that no matter what the nature of the particular job, be it manual, clerical, technical or administrative, it appears under the title of its eventual product. The industrial classification of coal mining then includes doctors, lawyers, and accountants. The occupational classification, on the other hand, looks only to the nature of the job, and not to the product, so that when we look later at the cross-tabulation of occupations across industries, we will see these same doctors, lawyers and accountants classed in professional occupations even though their industrial classification is as coal mining workers.[3]

The growth of so-called service employment has clearly revealed the inability of existing categories to give a rounded picture and to cope with change over time. New ones will emerge, as concepts catch up with reality: Gershuny and Miles, for example, propose a classification which divides service employment into service occupations, service products, and service functions.[4]

Despite these reservations, the typical worker, in so far as he or she exists, will be as much in the financial and professional occupations as in manufacturing industry. The former categories are themselves portmanteau ones, originally constructed precisely in order to aggregate small numbers of employees into groupings large enough to make statistical sense. But the essential point remains: the arenas of participation are as likely to be offices as factories; they will be peopled by white-collar and blue-collar workers in varying proportions, and they will be as likely to contain a sophisticated piece of computerized technology as a body press or assembly line.

Equally clear is the increased economic activity rate of *women* (Table 3). The influx of married women, who now make up over a quarter of the entire labour force, is especially significant, numerically and as a social phenomenon. The effect of their presence, at all levels, on patterns of power and decision-making is hard to estimate.[5] Some plausible if fairly crude psychologizing has suggested that women are disposed towards more collaborative and less hierarchical behaviour. On the other hand, female workers are also associated with other factors which have generally weakened labour's hand: low unionization rates, insecure part-time work, and sheer lack of confidence.[6]

Table 3 Economic activity rates (Great Britain) 1961−1981 (16 yrs. and over)

	Male		Female			
			Married		Non-married	
	Percentage of age-group economically active	Number (m.)	Percentage of age-group economically active	Number (m.)	Percentage of age-group economically active	Number (m.)
1961	86.0	16.1	20.7	3.9	50.6	3.9
1971	81.4	15.9	42.2	5.8	43.7	3.4
1981	78.1	15.9	49.5	6.7	43.6	3.7

Source: Social Trends 14 (HMSO, 1983).

Table 4 indicates the growth in *public-sector* employment, broadly understood as including public administration, health, education and welfare services, defence, and nationalized industries.[7] This ties in to a degree with trends already mentioned, in that the public sector contains a high proportion of service jobs; it also employs a substantially female labour force. The growth of this sector has spurred on white-collar unionization, since opposition to managerial unionization is far lower than in the private sector. It has, moreover, theoretical implications for the debate on democracy at work, raising the question of how far the rights of public-sector employees differ from those of their private-sector counterparts (see Chapter 7). The growth of the Welfare State, part of the general growth of the public sector, reminds us that it is impossible to divorce work from other areas of social life. In Scandinavia particularly, democratic regulation of social services is regarded as part of the move towards democratizing work. Similarly the Yugoslav system of enterprise self-management is integrally linked with the administration of local services such as schools and hospitals.

Table 4 The share of general government (national and local) in total employment in selected OECD countries 1960–1980 (percentage)

	1960	1971	1980
Austria	10.5	13.7	18.2
France	13.1	13.4	15.5
Japan	n/a	5.8	6.6
Netherlands	11.7	12.1	14.9
Sweden	12.8	20.6	30.7
UK	14.9	18.0	21.7
US	15.7	18.0	16.7

Source: OECD, *Employment in the Public Sector* (1982), table 1.

Finally there is the *temporal dispersion* of work. The rhythm of the working day and week has changed, so that work is now dispersed more widely throughout clock and calender time. Shiftwork has increased, usually to make more intensive use of capital equipment. Working hours generally have become more flexible, with a plethora of different systems for allocating worktime, sometimes enhancing employees' control over their own time, sometimes disrupting the rhythms of their lives inside and outside work. Allied to this is the growth of part-time and contract employment. Of the European Community's total work-force 9 per cent is now employed on a part-time basis, and the proportion rises to over 20 per cent in some countries. In the UK the figure is about 15 per cent (see Table 5 for details). The Community recognizes the implications of this for participation, in that it has produced a directive on part-time workers which requires that they should not be excluded from participating in bodies representing employees.[8] From one point of view part-time work offers welcome flexibility of employment. On the other hand, it also represents a means whereby employers can maintain a large penumbra of workers with minimal rights and little opportunity to influence their working conditions. The rise in short-term-contract work points in the same direction.

Table 5 Growth of part-time employment in Great Britain 1951–1981

Number of part-time workers (000)

	Male (part-time as percentage of all male workers)	*Female* (part-time as percentage of all female workers)
1951	45 (0.3)	754 (11.6)
1961	174 (1.2)	1,892 (26.1)
1971	584 (4.4)	2,757 (33.5)
1981	718 (5.9)	3,781 (41.6)

Source: Olive Robinson and John Wallace, 'Growth and Utilisation of Part-Time Labour in Great Britain', *Employment Gazette* 92:9 (Sept. 1984), 392.

In other words, just as the blue-collar male manufacturing worker is only one of a number of employee categories, so the eight-to-five, Monday-to-Friday image is increasingly atypical. That image— especially the total hours worked per week—was itself only fairly recently established. This fragmentation of time is as important in its implications for participation as many others of the trends referred to.

There are, of course, other shifts taking place, overlapping in various degrees with those listed above. Spatially, for example, the pattern of employment has been transformed, with regions which historically relied on older industries struggling to survive. But the trends already identified constitute the main features which give the work-force its current profile.

The union movement

How is the changing face of the work-force reflected in its collective representation through the trade union movement? We look briefly at its composition and organization, and also at its representative status.

Table 6 Membership of UK trade unions (000)

	Total membership	Percentage change from previous year
1976	12,386	
1977	12,846	+ 3.7
1978	13,112	+ 2.1
1979	13,289	+ 1.3
1980	12,947	− 2.6
1981	12,106	− 6.5
1982	11,593	− 4.2
1983	11,339	− 2.2

Source: Employment Gazette 92:1 (Jan. 1984).

In 1980, for the first time since 1958, total union *membership* fell significantly in the UK (Table 6). The decline mainly reflects the shrinkage in the total work-force, but the rate of unionization (the proportion of working people belonging to trade unions) dropped from 55.4 per cent in 1979 to 51 per cent in 1981,[9] and dipped below 50 per cent in 1983. The implications are considerable, especially since unions have conspicuously failed to maintain their subscription rates, and hence income, at anything like a constant proportion of members' wages. The recession has therefore struck both at the numbers of members and at the financial and organizational resources of the unions.[10]

To some extent unionization *patterns* follow the shifts in occupational and labour market participation patterns noted above. Obviously if there are more people working in service areas where white-collar unions operate, these unions will tend to grow, and the converse is true for declining blue-collar and manufacturing occupations. The trends are not even; unions have not always grown in direct proportion to the growth of the sectors in which they operate, and their growth has taken place at different rates. Nevertheless there has been a remarkable upsurge of union numbers in certain categories of worker, predominantly in the white-collar and managerial occupations. By 1979, about 40 per cent of all trade unionists were white-collar workers, compared with 32 per cent in 1968 and 23 per cent in 1948. However the impetus to union growth provided by white-collar unionization has petered out. Only the public-sector unions

(NALGO and NUPE)[11] maintained their growth in 1982, but even this is unlikely to continue for much longer.

Within the workplace, membership homogeneity is giving way to heterogeneity. A union such as NALGO includes a huge range of occupations within its membership. Clerical workers of the lowest grade can find themselves alongside a chief executive at branch meetings. This affects the character of collective action and the goals to which it is directed, as changes in the distribution of decision-making powers affect the union's members very differently.

Changes in the attitudes of union members towards their union and their elected representatives cannot be attributed solely to occupational shifts, though white-collar union members may have a more individualist orientation and be less likely to take part in collective activity than their blue-collar colleagues. Arguably, closed-shop agreements have to some extent both disguised and exacerbated the problems of the legitimacy of union representation, despite their obvious immediate advantages in ensuring high levels of membership. They put a higher premium on good communications between representatives and members, especially with the diminution of the check-off system,[12] which at least ensured some regular and direct contact, however cursory.

Unions vary widely in their internal structures, formally and informally. This makes any assessment of their representativeness and legitimacy highly problematic (witness the directly contrary criticisms levelled at all ranks of union representative, as being both too moderate and too militant, suppressing their members' aspirations and dragging them into unwanted action). Detailed research tends to reveal great diversity of machinery, ideology, and practice.[13] Shop stewards probably now have a harder task than in the past in establishing their credentials as the representatives of a broader collective organization with goals which transcend the immediate workplace. They are often seen as grievance-handlers, essentially there to resolve the problems of individual members. Emphasis on collective bargaining in the literal and traditional sense has been reduced, in favour of a stress on the 'insurance policy' advantages of union membership: legal advice, health and safety knowledge, and so on. It is uncertain how strong this trend is, and whether or not it reinforces the decentralization referred to earlier, but it places constraints on the options open to union representatives, at whatever level, in seeking to extend their share of decision-making.[14] Whatever the outcome of current legislative attempts to change their modes of governance, the unions face a continuing challenge to define and maintain the grounds of their legitimacy as genuinely collective bodies.

The consequences of these shifts in union membership and composition for workplace democracy are uncertain. As a general background, high unemployment and declining membership have sapped the union movement's morale and its resources, exposing its vulnerability to massive and sudden economic change. They inevitably weaken labour's ability to exert control, even if only of a defensive kind, against unilateral managerial decisions. The qualitative changes in the movement's composition have been more gradual, but have equal significance since strength does not lie in numbers alone. The ideological impetus which accompanied the original growth of unions and still provides much of its collective strength is less evident in the more modern unions. In the political constitutional sense fewer of the new big boys are officially affiliated to the Labour party (though that is itself not a sure indication of their ideological positions), and Conservative legislation passed in 1984 will almost certainly further loosen the links between the movement's political and industrial wings. Moreover, as a national organization, the TUC is experiencing increasing centrifugal pressures as the changing composition of the work-force disturbs its traditional structures, and divergent political views come to the surface. These divergences, it should be added, do not coincide with occupational divisions but cut across manual and white-collar, general and craft unions. The TUC has never been strong constitutionally; with the apparent collapse of the corporatist practices which gave it a national political role and the diminished degree of unified leadership from individual union chiefs, pressures towards fragmentation are not easily resisted.

There are, within the union movement, signs of major flux and a discernible trend towards organizational and ideological fragmentation. This bears some similarity to the decentralization of bargaining which took place in the 1960s—except that the contemporary political and labour market context is very different. The average representative, at whatever level, is better trained and can draw on more sophisticated back-up services, but has fewer collective resources to draw on. This is in the face of an increasingly complex organization of work.

Organizational structure

For people employed in a small garage, say, which is the sole asset of a local proprietor who works there himself, there is little ambiguity or complexity in the term 'workplace'. It is the physical spot where they present themselves most mornings, and where the authority to take decisions is to be found. For employees of ICI in Grangemouth, there may be a similarly stable physical construction into which they enter daily, but on the same day other employees will be entering into other locations spread throughout the world, and headquarters is 400 miles south in London. For other workers in other enterprises, the ultimate authority governing them is to be located, if it can be identified at all, somewhere overseas. Moreover, unlike the garage employee, whose fellow workers are all dealing with cars (even if only some actually put hand to axle grease), a very high proportion of workers are employees of the same organization as hundreds or thousands of others and yet the sole connection between them is precisely that they work for the same company. In the case of a conglomerate such as Wizco, whose business includes such diverse activities as printing, finance, the manufacture of plastic toys, and the management of large estates, it is difficult to conjure up a coherent image of what a Wizco employee is and what a Wizco workplace looks like.

Fewer firms now account for a greater proportion of output, own a larger number of plants, and employ larger numbers of people than ever before. A very substantial element of this increased concentration is accounted for by acquisitions and mergers. The firms which emerge from this process are typically multi-plant and involved in the production of a host of diverse goods and services, often in many different countries. So the gigantism of modern enterprises lies not in the physical size of their plants, most of which are small or medium size, but in their number and diversity. Already by 1972 the average giant manufacturing enterprise had 31,000 employees spread over 72 plants. In the previous fourteen years, the 100 largest enterprises had tripled the number of plants they owned, but the average number of employees in those plants had fallen by almost half, from 750 to 430.[15]

The contemporary workplace, then, may be the same size as—or even smaller than—its forerunner. The experience of work has perhaps not much changed in this physical respect. What has changed is the structure of the organizations of which the individual workplace forms part. The particular relevance of this from our point of view is that it substantially affects the ways in which decisions are made within organizations and within the constituent work-places, and this in turn affects the scope and the practice of employee participation. A 1979 publication on company organization and worker participation reported that 72 per cent of its sample companies were subsidiaries of larger concerns; two-thirds of the sample subsidiaries were controlled by their parent companies through directors which the latter had placed on their board; nine-tenths of the subsidiaries needed parent-company approval for major board decisions.[16]

The evolution is illustrated from a particular angle by Wigham, writing a history of the Engineering Employers Federation:

> In the old days a man on the spot was responsible only to himself. He might face bankruptcy but not dismissal by the heads of a conglomerate or multi-national company, with its headquarters in London or the US, preoccupied with short-term financial results. When a strike begins, according to one managing director, the distant owners say, 'Show them they can't have everything their own way.' In the second week of the strike, they say, 'Can't you get a reasonable compromise?' And in the third week, they say, 'For God's sake, get them back somehow.'[17]

Strategic authority now rarely resides on the spot. There is a continuing resultant tension between this and the aspirations and circumstances of those in the individual workplace, be they managers, union representatives, or rank-and-file employees. Managers may be frustrated by the lack of real discretion which they have even in exercising traditional management functions. In turn, shop stewards and union negotiators will find the scope of the agreements they can reach limited by absence of local managerial authority, and may strive to bypass it. Similarly, participative bodies dealing with issues alongside the collective bargaining channels will find themselves bumping up against limits imposed from above and elsewhere.

Naturally, there is a good deal of variation in the extent to which power in large organizations is devolved from or concentrated at the centre. Non-strategic issues can be as well settled at local level within a complex enterprise as in a single-plant structure. But the often labyrinthine nature of the decision-making process in contemporary organizations exacerbates the problems of democratic participation and accountability.

The number of plants and the complexity of decision-making are two features of contemporary organizations. A third is occupational diversity, which compounds the divisions produced by vertical hierarchy. Not only are there senior and junior levels of management (and departmental differentiation within management), but also professional, craft, skilled, and unskilled sections of the work-force, and these sections will have different interests and orientations in different parts of the organization. When these variegated occupations are brought together within a single conglomerate, the difficulties of establishing common interests and orientations are considerable, with substantial implications for the nature of collective decision-making. Nor is it only industry that is complex and occupationally diverse. National government employs fully qualified professionals, untrained labourers, and clerical officers with basic skills in the army, in social security offices, in research establishments, and so on.

The physiognomy of work continues to change. But the implications of occupational change for participation are often unpredictable. The military as an occupation is an inherently implausible candidate for democratization. Yet it provides one of the earliest examples of a formally structured representative system—and of such a system's problems. Over 300 years ago John Lilburne and the Agitators pressed for a democratic army, with some success: an Army Council was set up, with officer and soldier representatives from each regiment. Moreover, the representatives were accountable: in October 1647, Agitators of five cavalry regiments were recalled by their constituents under suspicion of having been corrupted by their officers, and replaced by new representatives. However, such a sudden degree of democracy could not be sustained and the participatory structure collapsed, amid acrimony and accusations of inefficiency.[18] Participative initiatives emerge from unlikely quarters, but the pace at which democratization can take place remains a highly relevant question.

2 Conflicts and powers

In this chapter we shall look at the concept of power, and link it to workplace relationships. The exercise of power is integrally tied up with conflict. But the character both of power relationships and of conflict varies widely. In subsequent chapters I shall illustrate this by reference to the way decisions are formulated on such specific topics as the work environment and the scope of occupational welfare.

Conventionally, the biggest single divide between approaches to democracy at work is discerned as between those—predominantly Marxists—who interpret it as an attempt to resolve the essentially irreconcilable interests of labour and capital, and the liberal view, which stresses the communality of interests between all sides of industry and sees industrial democracy as a means of harnessing energies to common ends. *Conflict or Cooperation?* was the title of a recent overview of developments within the UK,[1] and each pole can be illustrated by quotation. Thus Ernest Mandel writes, under the heading 'Participation, No! Control, Yes!':

Seeking to ensnare the workers' organizations and the workers in the trap of class collaboration, the employers pursue, from their side, a relentless class struggle. Trade unions and workers must refuse to make the slightest concession to the 'team spirit' the employers spread around. Workers must systematically refuse to take the slightest particle of responsibility for the management of capitalist enterprises and the capitalist economy. Inspection in order to challenge, yes; participation in, or sharing of, management, no.[2]

Compare this with the first of the principles of participation laid down by the Institute of Personnel Management:

Employee participation and involvement plans and strategies should take as their starting point the high degree of common interest and mutual interdependence which must exist in any successful organization between the employer, the employees and their representative organizations, the shareholders and, most significantly, the customer whom the organization seeks to serve.[3]

Conflict is indeed an endemic feature of society. It is, moreover, a *constantly recurring* characteristic of workplace relationships.[4]

I shall stress the precise applicability of the notion of 'recurrence'—in other words, conflict comes and goes, so that it is present in very variable forms at different times. There may be some to whom the idea that conflict is as pervasive as power is intuitively repugnant. To some extent this is a matter of verbal taste.[5] But it is important to clarify how the significance of conflict varies along a number of dimensions, which are themselves intertwined. By exploring these, we can better appreciate the kaleidoscopic nature of work-place relations.

In the first place, conflict may be *intense or mild*. Everyone is familiar with low-key disagreements which do little more than ruffle the surface of a relationship. The other end of the spectrum—the fight to the finish—is less universally familiar, in physical or economic terms. It is worth stressing that to reach a significant level of intensity some degree of equality must be present in the relationship of power, or there would be literally no contest.

Where is the cut-off point to be drawn, below which an action or situation is not conflictual? Rather than attempt to argue for a strict boundary, I would allow 'conflict' to include the apparently minor tensions which permeate everyday life, so that a continuum emerges running from all-engulfing strife to mild friction. In any case, however, when taken on its own this dimension yields no obvious dividing line between the significant and the insignificant.

The use of the dual term 'action or situation' above points the way to the second dimension: the extent to which conflict is *overt or latent*. Superficially this dimension may appear to coincide with the first one, since overt conflict could be expected to be more intense than latent conflict. But the converse can be argued: the deeper and more difficult to discern it is, the more menacing and powerful. There may be no strike on at the factory and very low levels of absenteeism and labour turnover, but in an economic recession can these be properly taken as signs of peace? The work-force may, on the contrary, be temporarily cowed by autocratic management, with conflict curbed only by external circumstances.

Thirdly, there is the nature of the *social unit* involved. Individuals can clash, whether or not they belong to the same class or group. Thus the finance and production directors may fall out at a board-room meeting, the head of a typing pool feud continuously with one of her girls, or an assembly-line car-worker vent his frustration by welding tool handles into fender compartments—causing 'mysterious, unfindable and eternal rattles'.[6] Small groups within the work-place regularly oppose each other. One study describes the mute struggle between planners, programmers, and machine operators for control over newly introduced technology, and at a different level within the same machine tool company the tensions between senior and middle management.[7] Earlier ones have analysed similar tensions in the infant days of the computer industry, or conflicting strategies within management personnel, to choose only two examples.[8] One can move rapidly up the scale to the national and even global levels, culminating in the types of tensions caused by the changing division of labour between countries and continents.[9]

These are unremarkable as parameters. But it is rarely made explicit how the use of them to assess the significance of conflict (as well as its probable outcome) depends very heavily on the *time-frame* adopted. The intensity, the proportion and pattern of overtness and latency, and the definition of the social units involved cannot be established without at least implicit reference to the period over which they take place.

This is in part a matter of simple duration. An insignificant spat between individuals consists only of a few harsh words. The majority of industrial disputes are unofficial and short-lived; they break the rules (of the union as well as the firm) and have some status as a direct challenge to authority, but they rarely develop into a sustained attack. High rates of absenteeism are a more indirect form of conflict, whilst high labour turnover rates represent a collective expression of discontent; to get an idea of the seriousness of either, one needs to know how long they last.

Other forms of conflict cannot be conceived of in terms of individual acts occurring at particular moments. In some senses, the tension between capital and labour is precisely what is reflected in the forms referred to above. But at a more abstract level it is not represented in those terms, but as a process which cannot be adequately grasped by inspecting empirical instances of opposition. Proponents of the end-of-ideology thesis argue that there is (now) no such opposition, that such conflicts as occur in industry stem from other, far more contingent, sources. But those who hold that there is such a tension vary widely amongst themselves in their view of its proximity to the surface and in the imminence of its eventual resolution. The more apocalyptic versions look to an early collapse of capitalism; others expect an eventual rupture but are more subdued in their approach—it will come, but probably not in their lifetimes. Such divergences can lead to diametrically different conclusions being drawn on the implications for political or industrial action.[10]

We can tie this more specifically to democracy at work, considered as a system whereby constituent members of an institution—the workplace—are able to act and organize in furtherance of their material or non-material interests. The concept of 'interest' and the perceived effectiveness of representatives in promoting those interests are both crucially affected by temporal considerations. Crouch points to the different time-horizons implied by the distinction between power as a goal and money as a goal, and how these differences can intensify the tension between unions and members.[11] He quotes Pizzorno:

The possibility of a gap between the interests of the represented and the interests of the representatives exists in the sacrifice of immediate benefits for the sake of future gains, when the union has the monopoly of legitimate interpretation of what is best, of what constitutes the 'true', that is long-term, interests of its members. In choosing power rather than immediate gains, it acquires positions which allow it more freedom of interpretation. The power of obtaining future benefits then becomes power over its own members.[12]

The time-frame which individuals or classes choose to use in their conception of their own interests is a vital determinant of how far and by whom they see those interests threatened and what measures they are prepared to take to promote or defend them. Nor is this restricted to labour. There is a distinct tension between capitalists with different time-perspectives: some will look for quick returns and immediate income, others for capital growth. This point assumes particular theoretical importance in the light of the rise of institutional shareholders, especially pension funds, whose interests may differ substantially from those of individual capitalists.

Cronin, seeking to explain the pattern of industrial conflict, criticizes the 'institutional' approach to industrial relations for adopting an inappropriate time-frame:

The peculiar rhythm of industrial strife, with its accent on discontinuity, is so unlike any notion of the development of industrial relations institutions, which is almost always continuous if not quite linear, and which generally proceeds by precedent, or by groping empiricisms, rather than by innovation, that the Clegg-Flanders model is of little use in understanding the history of strikes.

He goes on to suggest that explanations should be temporally 'symmetrical' to the problems they purport to explain.

Long-term questions deserve long-term answers, short-term ones short-term answers. Non-linear or irregular patterns must therefore be explained by reference to forces operative on a comparable timescale or to a combination of forces such that their interaction can explain temporal irregularity.[13]

Stated in this way the argument seems almost a truism, yet its implications are considerable, not least because it points to the possibility of time-scales which are themselves conflicting.[14]

In short, the notion of unanimity of interest cannot be sustained. Some of the conflict inherent in the workplaces of capitalist societies derives precisely from their capitalist nature. But the extent and character of such conflict need to be distinguished from other forms of conflict, whose origins are different or more complex and have little to do with questions of ownership or the domination of the market. Under almost any circumstances, there is at least a latent tension between different levels of decision-making, whether this be between the corporate centre of a capitalist firm and its subsidiaries, between elected administrations at central and local level, or between a socialist government and autonomously managed enterprises. Democratization may prevent or deflate some of the tensions. But it may provoke or expose others, or may push them below the surface, to re-emerge later. The redistribution of power, to which we now turn, is a volatile process.

Power

We talk regularly of the 'distribution' or the 'balance' of power. These are perfectly proper usages. Yet power is not a substance to be chopped up and weighed out in discrete lumps, like dough on a pastryboard. It is a characteristic of relationships between individuals, groups, and classes, as well as being the object of tension within and between them.

Table 7 Power and industrial relations

Concepts of power (Lukes)	Frameworks of industrial relations (Fox)
	Unitary (interests communal, conflict illegitimate)
One-dimensional (conflict observable)	
	Pluralist (interests divergent, conflict balanced)
Two-dimensional (conflict pre-empted suppressed)	
Three-dimensional (conflict covert and permeating)	Radical (interests opposed, conflict structural and unequal)

Something as pervasive and at the same time elusive as power has inevitably been the subject of extended debate.[15] We deal with it schematically. Steven Lukes's dimensional conceptualization is adopted (though not without reservations) as relating specifically to the process of decision-making. It dovetails neatly with Alan Fox's typology of industrial relations frameworks, providing a useful means of grasping the concept of power at the workplace. Table 7 summarizes the (approximate) parallelisms between the two.

The 'one-dimensional' view of power involves 'a focus on *behaviour* in the making of *decisions* on issues over which there is an observable *conflict* of (subjective) *interests* seen as express policy preferences, revealed by political participation'.[16] This can be rejected on almost every count: its preoccupation with overt behaviour, the narrow conception of a decision abstracted from the process which surrounds it, and the idea that conflict must be observable and preferences expressly articulated. The second dimension is introduced via the notion of 'non-decision-making'. A non-decision is 'a decision that results in a suppression or thwarting of a latent or manifest challenge to the interests of the decision-maker'. The two-dimensional view recognizes that barriers exist which impede public debate and prevent certain options from reaching public consciousness. Potential issues are aborted before they reach actuality.

This view was formulated originally in an analysis of urban politics in the USA, but no one would have much difficulty in relating it to workplace decision-making. Agenda manipulation, one of the most obvious examples of non-decision-making, is a familiar tactic within any organization, and the more bureaucratized the average workplace becomes, the more scope there is for this to occur. Nevertheless, non-decision-making is inadequate as an overall conceptualization: above all, it focuses too narrowly on decisions as events at a single moment, maintains a superficial view of the nature of conflict, and fails to recognize the way in which interests are really formulated.

Lukes therefore adds a third dimension. This stresses the covert side of power, the way it can be exercised without evident conflict, for example through accepted authority or manipulation. It extends the notion of decision-making back to include general control of issue formulation. The emphasis is clearly on hidden aspects, repudiating the view that if people feel no grievances, then they have no interests that are harmed by the use of power:

Is it not the most insidious exercise of power to prevent people to whatever degree, from having grievances by shaping their perceptions, cognitions and preferences in such a way that they accept their role in the existing order of things, either because they can see and imagine no alternative to it, or because they see it as natural and unchangeable, or because they value it as divinely ordained and beneficial?[17]

'Real' interests must be added to subjective and expressed ones.

The *unitary* view of industrial relations holds that there are common objectives and common values which bind together all participants. Conflict generated by organized opposition, typically trade unions, is illegitimate. Punishment is the appropriate response to transgression and managerial prerogatives may be enforced by coercion. (Parallels are drawn with other social groupings, such as the family, the football team, and the military unit, all seen as working together.) Such images regularly pervade discussions of participation, as the IPM quotation on p. 28 illustrates. Fox dismisses the unitary view summarily, regarding it as largely 'doublespeak' and out of touch with the reality of industrial life.

In the *pluralist* ideology the enterprise is seen as a coalition of individuals and groups, with their own aspirations and their own perceptions.

Thus the enterprise is seen as a complex of tensions and competing claims which have to be 'managed' in the interests of maintaining a viable collaborative structure . . . A certain amount of overt conflict and disputation is welcomed as evidence that not all aspirations are being either sapped by hopelessness or suppressed by power.[18]

The conflict, however, cannot be allowed to go beyond the bounds of reconcilability. Since a degree of opposition is legitimate, transgressors of the boundaries are regarded as nonconformists for whom punishment is not the appropriate response.

The key feature in Fox's account of the pluralist perspective is its assumption of a rough balance of power between the principal interest groups of society. This putative balance of power is the main focus of his criticisms of pluralism, which lead to the *radical* analysis. This 'asserts as its starting point a great disparity of power as between, on the one hand, the owners and controllers of economic resources and, on the other, those dependent on them for access to those resources as a means of livelihood'.[19] The focus is therefore on the inbuilt exploitation inherent in a society characterized by inequalities of ownership and control. Power derived from this structural source does not have to be openly exercised. Indeed, its exercise is least needed where the disparity between two groups is greatest. The legitimation of social institutions and mechanisms, the internalization of values and the confidence of superiority mean that no conspiracy is required for the existing distribution of power to be maintained.

Both Lukes and Fox, in different ways, stress four interrelated factors which are central to an understanding of power and the decision-making process at work. First, there are significant inequalities of power. Secondly, these inequalities are often structural and do not derive from personal characteristics. Thirdly, power relationships operate covertly as well as overtly. Fourthly, the exercise of power is most profound when it prevents the articulation or even formulation of opposing interests.

Neither of the two accounts can be regarded as definitive. Lukes's distinction of 'real' from subjective interests, for example, raises all sorts of theoretical and political hares: who, for instance, is to define employees' real interests: the boss, the personnel manager, the union official, the State, their spouses? Yet in conjunction they provide a springy jumping-off point for thinking about power in the workplace and about its Siamese twin, conflict. Some supplementary remarks are nevertheless needed.

Power relations at the workplace are not a direct function of underlying inequalities, unmediated by any intervening factors. It is more plausible, and conceptually adequate, to see power relations as a series of asymmetries.

Power relations in social systems can be regarded as relations of autonomy and dependence; but no matter how imbalanced they may be in terms of power, actors in subordinate positions are never wholly dependent, and are often very adept at converting whatever resources they possess into some degree of control over the conditions of reproduction of the system. In all social systems there is a *dialectic of control*, such that there are normally continually shifting balances of resources, altering the overall distribution of power.[20]

Emphasis on structural factors should not be allowed to obscure the plurality of power relationships operating at different levels and with different rhythms. Power relationships exhibit fluctuating degrees of inequality and instability, and power is exercised with varying degrees of ease and resistance, but these are not simple, fixed spectra. It is important neither to exclude those instances where a rough equality temporarily prevails, nor to disguise the variety of significant inequalities by insisting on a static dichotomy.[21]

It is arguable that the concept of power as a single entity lacks any explanatory force or theoretical significance. Minson, following Foucault, suggests that:

rendering power as an attribute with causal efficacy means that the outcomes of (power) struggles must either be deducible in advance from the power attributes of the forces of relations involved, or else beyond calculation altogether, inexplicable.[22]

He favours the plural use of 'powers', 'which might be conceived as *differential advantages* (or disadvantages) regarding the possibility of social agents being successful in realising certain objectives'. Where do these 'differential disadvantages' derive from? It may be useful simply to list the major *sources* of power (bearing in mind that power cannot be scooped up like water from a well):

- *Financial.* Wealth is obviously fundamental to the distribution of power. Capital bestows rights on shareholders (though not absolute rights, see Chapter 4). Departmental budgets influence the relative power of different managers. A union's power depends in part on the state of its coffers; and a company's capacity to resist on its reserves.

- *Legislative.* (a) *Direct.* Some countries have made extensive use of the law explicitly to promote democracy at work, notably West Germany, Sweden, and (more recently) France. These laws can cover institutional forms within public or private companies, new forms of organization (for example co-operatives), or specific rights of individuals. The force of such laws is distinctly variable. (b) *Indirect.* As well as general ownership rights, laws govern the scope for labour to organize, the rights of parties to litigate, individual and collective access to the media, and so on. At the extreme, any legislation influencing economic and social conditions affects the general balance of power.

- *Formal position.* Authority deriving from a particular position within an organization also takes direct and indirect forms. For example, in decisions governing company affairs generally, a managing director derives power directly from his official position; if he participates in a consultative committee on formally equal terms with the other members, he will still derive power from his position as Managing Director.

- *Expertise.* Possession of technical knowledge is often a significant factor. Numerous studies, for instance of Yugoslavian and Israeli democratic initiatives, show how technically qualified employees participate more fully than other categories.[23] The expertise may be social as well as technical; recognized or not; genuine or merely reputed.

- *Market position.* The ability of employees—at whatever level—to gain employment elsewhere shapes their power, individually or collectively, as does the ability of the organization to replace them—hence the long-standing debate on the impact of the 'reserve army of labour'. Subsumed under this heading is the opportunity for groups or individuals to improve their market position, for instance through training.

- *Technology.* The work of some segments of the work-force is directly subject to the technology employed. Others are relatively autonomous or in an ambivalent relation: their work is closely geared to the technology yet it gives them great disruptive power. Since technology does not drop fully formed from the sky, this heading includes control over the choice and design of the technology itself.[24]

- *State policy.* The complexion of the government in office is a potentially important source of power, as are the activities of the components of the State machinery. These are strongly inter-related with other items in this list: the State can act as a source of finance, law, expertise, and so on. This is in addition to its own role as an employer, fostering or opposing participative initiatives.

- *Ideology.* A prevailing national ideology, for instance of egalitarianism or, on the other hand, of meritocracy, can be a major source of power. Alternatively the ideology can be restricted to a particular class or group, forming a strong part of its identity.

Few if any of these sources are straightforward in their implications. A clearly formed and revered ideology may be a source of weakness as well as strength to a particular class if it induces blinkered conservatism. Or an apparently favourable law may 'demobilize' a group, inducing it to use a juridical rather than organizational strategy, with poor results. But although no easy matrix emerges, the identification of sources enables us to get our bearings on the way power is exercised. This is given concrete illustration in Chapters 4 and following.

In summary, the relationships between individuals and between classes embody fluctuating inequalities of power which derive from a range of sources. Often the inequalities are structural, in that they are a feature of the system within which the agents operate, rather than of the agents themselves. The introduction, implementation, and development of any initiative towards greater democracy will reflect these inequalities and the struggle to correct them, exhibiting recurrent tensions and conflicts. Such conflicts are obviously of varying dimensions.

In analysing their incidence and significance we should be aware of the multiplicity of potential interpretations afforded by different temporal perspectives.

In the long run, the interests of capital and labour may prove to be incompatible, leading to a cataclysmic change in economic and social structures. But how long is the long run? Is there an even longer run? Are all the short runs only smaller units of the long run? And in the mean time are not other conflicts equally or more significant? Restricting ourselves to the workplace as a specific arena of social conflict, we can identify a whole series of oppositional pairings: producers vs. consumers, owners vs. managers, employers vs. employees, political democracy vs. industrial democracy, safety vs. productivity, long-term planning vs. short-term tactics. Yet the conflict is never head-on at exactly 180 degrees, and rarely if ever confined to two parties alone. Let us acknowledge, for example, that there is tension between democracy and economic efficiency (however defined)—but so there is between efficiency and one of democracy's antitheses, autocracy. The forms conflict takes are so diverse and themselves change so substantially that they cannot all plausibly be related back to a single opposition. Proteus eludes Procrustes: the changing plurality of conflict cannot be crammed into the dichotomizer's framework.

3 Stages, cycles, and rhythms

The purpose of this chapter is not to give a historical account of developments in participation, but to convey a sense of the diversity of their paths and origins. Some burst out like shooting stars, appearing from nowhere and quickly fizzling out. Others glimmer away permanently in the background, becoming prominent only under particular atmospheric circumstances.

The character of a social phenomenon such as participation changes continuously, acquiring and sloughing off parts and varying in the compactness of its composition. It might be identified closely with board-level representation, so that the idea of worker directors forms a dense molecule round which the rest of the concept clusters. At other times, it is more loosely structured, covering a range of institutional and non-institutional practices. Some elements temporarily or permanently lose contact altogether with the central mass, or float off to the periphery; it could be argued that this has been the case in the past with profit-sharing, though that has now loosely reattached itself as part of the shift towards economic democracy.[1]

The unstable character of the phenomenon is evident from the way in which its constituent elements follow different trajectories. Thus one form may be given a sudden and specific impulse, as the Whitley Report on relations between employers and employed gave to joint consultative committees after the First World War. Similarly the 1974 Health and Safety Act gave impetus to joint health and safety committees (see Chapter 6), but in this case the impulse, though specifically provided by an act of legislation, was the product of a long process of intermittent pressure and delay. The EEC's Fifth Directive on worker participation has at the time of writing been in draft form for twelve years. The length of the gestation derives from a mix of cultural variance, political rivalry, bureaucratic cumbersomeness, and hard lobbying by business interests. In its course, the notion of participation has been through several mutations, passing from representation on supervisory boards to a plural conception embracing several other alternatives: elected works councils, consultative systems set up through collective bargaining, and representation via elected non-executive directors on a unitary board.

To take another, less institutional, example, the idea of quality circles[2] as an instance of participation at workgroup level was canvassed in the US in the early 1960s, an era of rapid economic expansion and high consumer demand. The idea disappeared in the scramble to get goods out of the factories and into the shops, with comparatively little importance attached to quality control. There was some incentive to promote participation as a way of retaining labour, but economically it made more sense to look to high productivity and high wages to keep business rolling. So quality circles submerged, swam across the Pacific Ocean and back, and resurfaced a decade and a half later as an import from the US's successful competitor, Japan. In the face of stagnant or declining demand, an essential marketing element is a good reputation for fault-free products. Competition stoked by recession shifts the emphasis from quantity to quality, and up comes a revamped model of an old participative initiative.

A historical perspective helps us to understand the relative strengths of different trends and to capture their waxings and wanings. More than that, it may help to reveal regular patterns of human behaviour (for example managerial responses to labour market pressures) or of institutional life (for example the growth and decay of formal consultative bodies), and conversely to pick out events or processes which mark a significant departure from previous experience.

Evolution by stages

The evolutionary model sees change as progression through a series of gradual and incremental stages. The phenomenon under inspection—be it a species or a social organism—unfolds along a particular path. It not only changes but acquires qualities that make its later forms superior to earlier ones. In the workplace context, such an approach would describe the growth and consolidation of employees' rights and also diminished managerial authoritarianism. Conditions are continuously ameliorated without major disturbance to the social structure.

In a loose sense the evolutionary view shares many of the characteristics of the unitary frame of reference outlined in the previous chapter. Progress is a matter of the rational and ordered pursuit of common goals. It need not be smooth; it may pass through stages of consolidation, delay, or even retrenchment. But there is a teleological

singularity of direction. Industrial society has its shady and tyranni-
cal past and retains some murky corners, but these are being progressively swept clean.[3]

It is difficult to muster substantial empirical support for this view
as applied to the democratization of work. Shifts in the distribution of
power have been too spasmodic and their character too diverse to be
smoothed into any but the longest of long-term evolutionary paths.
From the last century onwards, putative moves towards greater
democracy have often proved ephemeral or ambiguous in their
impact. The shortcomings of State ownership, managerial mani-
pulativeness, the unpreparedness of worker representatives smoothly
to assume new duties and responsibilities, the unaccountable rest-
lessness of finance capital—these and many other factors make it
implausible to see democratization as a steady trend, despite the
enthusiasm of its more evangelical proponents. Above all, however,
recurrent economic turbulence discredits the evolutionary view. In
the recessionary 1980s the judgement of the Bullock Committee on
industrial democracy sounds almost anachronistic (even allowing for
the fact that the Report had the political objective of creating a
favourable climate for the adoption of its proposals):

In such cases [important investment decisions] it becomes increasingly difficult for employers to deny the right of these employees, not only to have their
interests taken into account by management, but also to have an opportunity
for active involvement in the decision-making process. Such responses on the
part of companies may in part be a recognition of social responsibility or of
democratic principles, but they are also evidence of the practical reality that
if a company neglects to make provision for such involvement, employees are
now in a position, through the strengthening of trade union organisation and
power, to resist the implementation of changes that threaten their livelihood
and security.[4]

Less than a decade later, and even in companies with a reputation for
benevolent industrial relations, employees are poorly placed to assert
their particular interests in the face of national and international
upheaval. There are material forces that impose themselves dis-
ruptively, whatever the drift of political ideology or social
will.

Cycling

The cycle is a common image, especially in economic parlance.
Applied to participation, the cyclical view holds that there are
periods when an apparent surge of democratization occurs, but these

are consistently followed by the restoration of the status quo ante in the distribution of power.

This can be portrayed as almost a natural process, which occurs without the help of human intervention. Organizations must change and one form of change will be towards greater participation, but this cannot be sustained as the evolutionary model would have us believe. The authority structure will therefore resume approximately its original shape. More purposive interpretations hold that participation initiatives can be shown historically to be a tactic of employers compelled to respond to threats to their managerial authority. The initiatives are put forward very much in a unitary framework, stressing the common interests of employer and employee and projecting participation as a combined effort for mutual benefit. Once the threat to managerial authority evaporates, the initiative either dies away or is actively relegated to insignificance.

Profit-sharing schemes, for example, have a long historical pedigree. They grew rapidly in the latter part of the nineteenth century (88 were introduced between 1889 and 1892, compared with 40 in the previous fifteen years), clearly related to industrial unrest and high employment levels.[5] They were thus largely devices for defusing trouble and for retaining labour loyal to the company, rather than altruistic moves to share out financial power and rewards more equitably. At least six of the early initiatives were quite explicitly anti-union, introduced to prevent the formation of any collective opposition. With the decline of unrest, profit-sharing faded. It re-emerges periodically (and is enjoying a contemporary resurgence), but so far without lasting effects.

The nineteenth-century spurt in profit-sharing is the first of four cycles which make up one version of the cyclical model.[6] The second arrives at the end of the First World War. Pressures on employers had been generated by the growth of union membership (from 2 million in 1911 to 5 million in 1919), by a combination of industrial and political disaffection (in Sheffield and Clydeside especially), and by the emergence of threatening political doctrines such as guild socialism. The Whitley Committee was set up in response to this. Its final proposals, for a three-tier system of joint committees in each industry, at national, district, and workshop level, did not take immediate root. Although they were designed originally for the private sector, the government found itself having to take the lead by establishing them first in the public sector, where indeed they have always played a more prominent role. At their peak the committees covered 3.5 million employees, but the majority had already run out of steam by 1926, when only 47 out of 98 schemes were still in existence.[7] The depression had set in, unions were on the retreat, and the pressure was off the employers.

During the Second World War, the pattern of employers responding to the threat of nascent worker power and then soft-pedalling is repeated, though in different form. There was neither the same level of industrial and political militancy nor the external source of revolutionary ferment that Russia had been in 1917/18. But there was a desperate need to keep production going. The response was the creation of Joint Production Committees, some 4,500 of which were estimated to be in existence by December 1943. These were not to be regarded as negotiating bodies, but as means of promoting output and ensuring its continuity. Through them workers were to gain an understanding of the problems of management. By 1948, however, their numbers had dropped below 600, reflecting or even anticipating the dissipation of the co-operative spirit generated by the war.

There is a tail to this cycle. In January 1948, the government, facing particular economic difficulties in part as a consequence of the fuel crisis, attempted to revive interest in joint consultation. The recommendations produced by a National Joint Advisory Council were based on voluntary initiatives but never took deep root, and by the early fifties interest in participation had diminished, submerged in the rising tide of material prosperity.

The fourth period selected begins with the productivity bargaining which was prominent in the early 1960s. It is characterized by the ending of substantial and apparently assured economic growth. Diminishing profits led to a search for solutions to the weaknesses suddenly appearing in British industry. Productivity agreements were the response, allied to a pragmatic recognition of the need to involve unions in at least some of the decision-making processes.[8] Their rise and fall form a separate cycle within the larger cycle of the contemporary period.

The value of the cyclical model is that it demolishes the plausibility of a steady march towards an agreed objective of workplace democracy. It establishes instead that there are periods in history when the tide is running in favour of participation, and periods when it is pulling against it. History dutifully records the fact that initiatives were taken, and over time these build up into an impressive portfolio of investments in participation. But the performance of the portfolio over time—the sustained value of the stock after it has been launched on the market—is less regularly charted, and shows a different picture. Cumulative calculations should be balanced by the subtraction of ephemeral initiatives; only then should the sum total of progress be established.[9]

Moreover, the cyclical approach encourages consideration of motive forces. The provisional ceding of power may be a calculated manœuvre, a short-term concession made as the price to pay for avoiding a transfer of ownership or other radical forms of power redistribution. The exploitation of time itself as a device for preserving the status quo is often a key tactic.

There are, however, inadequacies in the cycle as a model for tracing trends and counter-trends in industrial democracy. By stressing the repetitive pattern of events the cyclical model muffles the diverse rhythms of change. Some versions exhibit a functionalist tendency to exaggerate capital's ability to maintain the status quo, diminishing both the industrial and political impact of labour and the system's inbuilt dynamism and propensity to change. Having rescued us from conceiving of trends as unidirectional—always upward—it suggests instead only two directions, up and down, instead of the swirling plurality which more closely resembles reality. A different version holds that managements are not in fact successful in their attempts to head off unrest by introducing participation. The implication is that neither the initiatives nor their demise are of much significance, since they fail to resolve the system's basic contradictions. Such an approach avoids the functionalism of the first, but it deprives the events of substance: they are insubstantial camouflage, transparently papering over systemic cracks.

A cycle necessarily implies the repetition of an ordered sequence, and this raises two questions: what degree of similarity does there have to be between the events of different cycles, and how far can they deviate from each other in their sequences? It is doubtful whether even in broad terms the same sequence can be shown to occur in successive periods: in some cases participation initiatives are a last-ditch response to a crisis, in others a forward-looking attempt to ensure a continued tranquillity of industrial relations. Secondly, the periodicity—the *duration* of the sequence—has to be fairly clearly established if the clear image of a cycle is to be maintained. Marx conceived of crises repeating themselves in cyclical fashion each decade, the material basis for this repetition being the wearing out, replacement, and expansion of the machines which constitute the means of production. Such quantitative specificity is unnecessary, but some degree of temporal equivalence between different periods is needed if their characterization as cycles is not to seem arbitrary.

Management initiatives towards participation may usually be provisional and short-term. But there is no logical reason why this should be so, especially if the incorporative rationale—that participation functionally integrates workers into the system—is assumed to carry any weight. By the mid-1920s the steam behind post-war initiatives had evaporated in the face of the slump, and the labour movement was left in disarray by the defeat of the General Strike. Why then did Sir Alfred Mond, an arch-capitalist from the chemical industry, strike up a variation on the participation theme, initiating talks with labour representatives on the basis that employers and employed can find many areas of common ground? Mond–Turnerism (Mond's counterpart as leader of the trade union representatives was Ben Turner, President of the National Union of Textile Workers) was not strong enough to establish corporatist joint decision-making securely, but it does make it difficult to see the latter half of the 1920s simply as a time of reaffirmed employer unilateralism. Mond was not under pressure from a well-organized labour force to concede parts of his authority, nor (in slump conditions) from product-hungry consumers to keep output up even at the expense of managerial control. He may have been 'an exception among employers in that his interest in participation as a means useful in the long term to curb industrial unrest persisted in this period of industrial problems'.[10] His initiatives do not, however, imply that he was less of a capitalist than the others. It simply means that he was more far-sighted (or, to put it more neutrally, had a longer planning horizon) than them.[11]

Without subscribing explicitly to the cyclical view, McCarthy concluded that the only way in which participative bodies such as consultative committees can maintain significance as an organ of joint decision-making is by changing into a bargaining forum.[12] Otherwise, he argued, they would regularly follow the pattern of degeneration into triviality. This dictum attained almost axiomatic status in the 1960s and 1970s, at a time when trade unionism was growing rapidly, bargaining spread, and the number of negotiators at all levels mushroomed. Yet almost all the recent evidence shows consultative structures as persisting even during this period, and developing in a complex but broadly complementary relationship with collective bargaining.[13] Fluctuations, of course, in both content and strength; but no closed circle of rise and fall.

Rhythms

The promotion or suppression of industrial democracy cannot be plausibly attributed to managerial planning alone, to trade union vigour, nor to any other single source. There is a range of forces which push and pull at the shape of decision-making, from different angles and each with its own rhythm. The rhythms may coincide, accentuating each other, or conflict, in which case they may either cancel each other out or provoke a catalytic change. Given the indeterminacy of each of the rhythms it is unlikely that they will repeatedly interact in the same way, and this is the dominant reason why the image of a cycle is inappropriate.

There is no inexorable tide in favour of democratization. But perhaps the conventional connotation of the metaphor is wrong, rather than the image itself. If we extend the time-frame to include the ebb phase, the image of a smooth flow forward crumbles away. And if we broaden our perspective, it shows ebbs and flows occurring simultaneously at different places. The effect is not purely repetitive since tidal movement affects the contours of the coastline and the sea bottom, sometimes dramatically. The changes wrought range from gradual erosion to the cataclysmic effect of neap-tides. Tides are not neutral phenomena. They do not move in a vacuum, but impinge, often severely, on their environment and those who inhabit it. They have an element of repetition but no symmetry. As a symbol of rhythm, they suffice.

Neither here nor anywhere else can a complete picture be painted of rhythms in the democratization process. An extended historical perspective yields different conclusions to those of a more narrowly focused approach. But we can sketch out examples of fluctuations in the behaviour of the major agents involved. Alongside employers, already noted as significant parties, must be ranged governments and organized labour. The activities of all three shape and are shaped by broad economic movements. A few remarks on each must suffice, dealing with them only at the broadest level (and largely ignoring variations between labour markets, or between different levels of government, or between individual unions).

Economic activity and employment

Fluctuations in the demand for goods and labour influence the probability of democratization. When consumer demand is high, management may concede on issues on which they might otherwise have resisted. The concession is then consolidated into custom and practice, or into institutional form, with differing degrees of subsequent slippage back towards the status quo ante. On the other hand, a booming consumer economy also means that employees are likely to be making progress materially, and this is commonly thought to reduce their incentive to press for a different planning order.

The impact of the labour market is less ambivalent. Full employment and a tight labour market strengthen labour's ability to exert pressure on managerial authority. Employers may respond to this pressure directly, or seek to pre-empt it. The pressure is not necessarily overtly conflictual in character. Where good industrial relations prevail,[14] a participation initiative can build on them with the active support of both management and labour. It remains true that joint decision-making is a more plausible venture when there is some rough equality of power. Given the inherent advantages of capital, labour tends to come closest to that equality at times of full employment.

It is the *equalizing* potential of economic conditions which is important and this can occur through levelling down as well as levelling up. Severe economic problems may constrain management's freedom of manoeuvre to such an extent that they are willing to take the risk—previously judged unacceptable—of inviting labour to share more fully in decision-making.[15] Nevertheless, there is no symmetry between the poles of economic boom and survival conditions, since the latter are less conducive to experimentation and risk. Boom conditions increase the possibility that each of the interest groups involved can find some advantage in change. Middle managers are a group most typically threatened by participation, but an expanding economy enhances their career prospects. Shop stewards can continue to secure wage increases for their members and to guard job security. On balance, therefore, times of full employment and economic growth are more likely to witness active interest in participation.

The form that interest takes may have little to do with institutional forms of participation. The 1950s and early 1960s saw no widespread movement in that direction, but rather a significant accretion of shopfloor power through a decentralized shop steward system. The Donovan Report of 1968 aptly characterized this as the informal system of industrial relations.[16] There was little pressure at the time for alternative forms of participation, which would naturally have been seen as rival rather than complementary.

Yet such a system could not remain static, as the example of British Leyland shows. The company was itself not successful, but general economic and labour market conditions combined with weak management to enable shop stewards to win a very substantial degree of informal control at shop-floor level, though not over strategic decisions. By the 1970s conditions had changed. BL then introduced a complex system of formal participation at the very time that the economy was flagging, the car industry suffering more than most, and BL in particular trouble. The confluence partly accounts for the failure of the scheme, which further weakened the informal power of the shop stewards.

Since then, labour market conditions have deteriorated dramatically, greatly eroding the power of most sections of organized labour to claim any enhanced share in decision-making, at whatever level. The response of employers to their strengthened position has been mixed; some have sought to turn the clock back to the days of management by fiat, whilst others have looked forward, seeking to secure themselves in the future by initiating systems of communication and consultation at a time when they are able to control their character themselves. Differences in response can be attributed to variations in horizon as well as in history.

The role of government

Clearly both political administrations and the machinery of State are often influenced, overtly or covertly, by the power of employers and capital generally.[17] Recent discussions of the State have underlined how its various components function to some extent independently of the elected administration, making effective direct political control more difficult.[18] But unless, with Lenin, one views the State as merely the committee of the bourgeoisie, it is worth reflecting on what sort of impact fluctuations in governmental activity and attitudes have on the growth, subversion, or suppression of participation.

The relationship between State policy and producer sovereignty has long been a focal point of political theorizing. It was most prominent in the opposition between the guild socialists such as G. D. H. Cole who supported the maximum degree of producer autonomy, and the Webbs and their followers who wanted to see a stronger State role. But governmental activity in relation to democracy at work has usually been shaped less by specific considerations of effective decision-making and more by external factors, whether they be economic social—or military. For in the first half of this century, State policy in the field was broadly structured by the world wars. During the wars, the primacy of national survival was used to counter pressures for workplace democracy, except where this was seen as functional to economic or military output. After each war, there were attempts to combine the task of economic reconstruction with a response to popular demands for a new social order, including the extension of democracy at work. Judgements on the sincerity and effectiveness of these attempts vary.[19] We can only note that the focus and goals of governments are distinct, though not independent, from those of other interests. In and out of war, the rhythms of State activities— that is, their duration and intensity—both coincide and conflict with other social institutions.

A few examples must suffice. We have seen that the Whitley Committee was set up in 1917 largely in response to industrial militancy. It may have served the employers' purposes by defusing potentially explosive pressures, but it is difficult to see the Whitley initiative as a deliberate tactic on their part, encouraged so long as it served their purposes and then quietly dropped. They never showed much positive enthusiasm for the proposals, and implementation took place mostly in the public sector. The State can be said to have acted quasi-autonomously, instituting machinery which has survived unspectacularly but surprisingly well, given the lack of initial support from its employer and trade union godparents.

The 1945 Labour government had a substantially different ideology from its predecessors. The measures of nationalization it introduced were far more controversial and could in principle have heralded a major advance in industrial democracy. They did not, partly because the government leaned to the view that the goal of nationalization was to promote efficiency, as Herbert Morrison believed, rather than to further democracy, as Bevan and others did.[20] But a major vehicle for industrial democracy had had its starting-handle turned by the State, even if the clutch was never very firmly engaged and the resulting fumes from an idling motor cast rather a pall over the area.[21]

The devastation of war provided something of a *tabula rasa* on which to sketch out new designs. Peacetime politics has tended to be more concerned with observing existing conventions and keeping the show on the road. The Conservative administrations of the 1950s paddled along in the warm current of economic growth. The temperature was raised in 1964 by a Labour government primarily concerned with developing central planning. Faced with major structural economic problems it sought to regulate union activity through legislation, with no serious attempt to link this to institutional reform of workplace decision-making. There were inadequate efforts to prepare the way by converting union leaders to the policy, let alone the rank and file. The result was that an attempt to initiate and execute significant organizational change by snap political decision came up painfully against a union movement which had its feet braced firmly on the tradition-hallowed ground of collective bargaining.

The 1970 Conservative government took no significant steps to promote participation in the workplace. However it did continue the corporatist ethos of the 1960s by carrying on with consultative institutions at national level. It did not reject the idea that representatives of labour as well as capital should be involved in some areas of policy formulation, through bodies such as NEDC or the MSC, and thus continued a tradition which was to be sharply rejected when the Conservatives returned to power at the end of the decade.

Early in the lifetime of the next Labour government (1976), a specific political initiative was taken with the setting up of a Committee of Inquiry to consider the means of introducing board-level representation (see Chapter 8). Naturally the initiative did not come out of the blue (though an accident of parliamentary procedure was involved) and its origins can be traced directly back to the 1960s.[22] The Committee's report, published in 1977, provoked howls of opposition from business interests. It had only lukewarm and divided support from the labour movement. In the event, the vicissitudes of parliamentary democracy pushed Labour into a pact with the Liberals, part of the price being a substantial watering down of the original proposals. Never well nourished, the animal was killed off by the return in 1979 of a Conservative government which proved not evolutionary but 'creationist' in its assertion of the fundamental rights of capital.

It is evident that fluctuations in political activity do not depend only on variations in the political colour of central government. They are shaped by the presence and quality of medium- or long-term planning capacity, the magnitude and predictability of changes in the world economy or in specific industries, simple tradition, and so on—all in addition to the relationships with capital and labour. There are complicating factors generated by the operations of the political machine: internal party manœuvrings, electoral considerations, and the activity of parties in opposition. Moreover, governments are, of course, not only national. Since the days of G. D. H. Cole municipal government has had an association with self-government in industry, and the London Passenger Transport Board was a pioneer in the 1930s. Today, several local authorities are taking initiatives (such as Local Enterprise Boards) designed to promote regional economic activity but often also industrial democracy, for example by stipulating that companies who benefit from financial aid should involve union representatives in their strategic planning. Such initiatives may run directly counter to the ideology of the central administration—indeed, their intensity may be closely associated with the degree of opposition to the national government. The rhythms of political activity, even narrowly conceived, are multiple, and not always orchestrated.

For a comparative instance of fluctuation in State activity, we can turn to Yugoslavia. Self-management is a pervasive social and political theme there, and it is not surprising that the role of the State is inextricably intertwined with enterprise politics. There is recurrent tension between the two, with successive swings of the pendulum taking place against a changing set of economic and social circumstances.[23] The initial impulse of self-management came from Yugoslavia's expulsion from the Comintern in 1948 and a revulsion against Stalinist forms of centralized planning. Through the next two decades there was a growth in enterprise autonomy, but this generated inequalities between and within enterprises and tensions between different levels of planning units. In the 1970s there was therefore a fresh attempt to redefine the allocation of economic and political responsibilities between enterprises and federal and local governments. Shifts in State policy have thus reflected the tension, favouring sometimes central planning, at other times a greater reliance on market mechanisms and self-managed enterprise autonomy.[24]

Organized labour

The activities and attitudes of organized labour are obviously linked both to economic conditions and to governmental practice, as the previous sections have already made clear. Unions may respond to boom conditions and tight labour markets simply by pushing for higher wages; or they may also seek to make strategic inroads on managerial prerogatives, normally through the extension of collective bargaining but also through exerting pressure on governments to adopt policies or pass legislation favourable to them. In the British context, with its high degree of decentralization and relatively weak central union federation, it is very difficult to generalize historically on union attitudes to participation. On the one hand, established unions in the heavy industries have a long tradition of collective bargaining, which they may be reluctant to abandon or modify. On the other hand, many of these same industries (steel, coal, railways) are now in public hands, with extensive consultative arrangements.[25] We have already noted the growing strength within the TUC of public-service unions, for whom traditional bargaining over the distribution of the economic surplus has never been appropriate— except in the sense that a booming economy means higher State revenues.

Union behaviour in relation to democratization has varied along a number of dimensions. First, there have always been divergent ideological opinions on the primacy of public ownership as a precondition of true industrial democracy. Secondly, perceptions of bargaining strength and the use to be made of such strength naturally vary, as industries rise and fall and the demand for trade skills does likewise. Thirdly, some unions are more committed than others to the TUC as a central institution with a duty to articulate the views of the union movement, including those on the issue of democracy at work. Related to this is the notoriously complex relation between organized labour and the State. Whilst there has been historically a close relationship between trade unions and the political Labour party in the UK (and in other countries, such as Denmark and Sweden), the relationship has fluctuated in its closeness. Moreover, collaboration at the top through corporatist structures does not ensure co-operation lower down,[26] and the longer-term consequences of unlegitimated collaboration can provoke a reaction which is immediately damaging and whose consequences may be lasting—an obvious example being the continued wage restrictions of the late 1970s.

Certainly unions fluctuate in their relation to participation, but they can rarely be convincingly portrayed as wholly passive, as the managerial manipulation doctrine would suggest in its purest form. It was the union movement, led by Jack Jones, that generated much of the impetus behind the attempt to introduce worker directors, and there are numerous other examples of labour taking the initiative. Conversely, unions have also prevented the implementation of participation schemes, or effectively· undermined them and rendered them unworkable.[27]

Organized labour in other countries has a rather less diverse set of attitudes. In the US, unions have maintained a fairly consistent view of participation over a long period of time. Though determined to maintain the role of collective bargaining, and to some extent successful in having it legally underpinned, they have eschewed a share in company decision-making.[28] Yet unions are seeking to assume at least part of the most important managerial role of all, the control of capital, through participation in the management of pension funds. European unions, notably in France and Italy, have been characterized by a higher degree of political theory in their approach to participation, especially in so far as it is interpreted as 'managing capitalism'. Yet political changes in the two countries have impelled the unions towards a more pragmatic position. In France, the advent of a Left government in 1981 raised the expectations of both major union confederations, the CFDT (which has long supported a highly decentralized conception of *autogestion*, or self-management) and the Communist CGT. They have received legislative support for enhanced power at the workplace, through the *'lois Auroux'*. But economic turbulence has muted the impact of these new rights and the extension of public ownership has done little to shift the balance of power. Both union bodies are being forced to rethink the relations between economic facts, political theory, and democratic practice.

In Italy, the unions have no politically sympathetic government as an interlocutor. They resemble the British in having a relatively decentralized system of collective bargaining, and have chosen to press for planning agreements and the release of information to workers councils at enterprise level. This pursuit of piecemeal gains is not unconnected with the tactical evolution of the Italian Communist party, aware that a policy of transforming workplace relations by national political action is unlikely to be successful.

In short, sections of the labour movement have supported and opposed participation initiatives with greater or less vigour at various times, to say nothing of the variation between countries. The variations can be due to divergences of interpretation as to the impact on collective bargaining, to changes in leadership, to the sudden emergence of new priorities, or to banal factors such as the incompetent handling of a conference resolution. Certainly there are trends to be discerned, but no single pattern. Goodrich's confidence in the onward march of labour was obviously misplaced, but he appreciated the complexity of the challenge posed to unions by the prospect of greater control, and this complexity is reflected in the diversity of their subsequent responses.

Social trends

We are left, then, with a very complex picture of shifting patterns. The historical perspective disabuses us of any notion of inexorable progress towards greater particpation. This chapter has concentrated primarily on economic trends and agents. But there is a further underlying current which can be simply stated. Outside the workplace, deference and authoritarianism are less and less common. In a whole range of social institutions the idea of unquestioning obedience is disappearing—in schools, in families, even in the army, where although full democracy is unlikely there is a greater sophistication in the way authority is exercised, a kind of socialization of command.

Inseparable from this trend is the growth in exposure to knowledge. A far higher proportion of young people carry on with formal education until their late teens, and adult education is increasingly recognized as an integral part of life, not a marginal activity. Informal learning has exploded, especially with the advent of the mass media. People know how other people behave, that things can be handled differently, that there is (probably) no single best way. They have in front of them a huge range of that highly subversive commodity: alternatives. Short of some remarkable turnabout in social mores (the triumphant success of fundamentalist religious groups, perhaps), the pressure exerted by these external trends on the structure of authority at work will not evaporate. This is far from saying that it will be in an unequivocally democratic direction—a decreasingly deferential populace can still give its support to a charismatic ideologue—but it is a force which makes it above all difficult to maintain the status quo. How long it will take to make a fundamental impact is uncertain. As with all the other features discussed, evaluation of its significance depends upon the time-scale within which it is viewed.

4 Self-ownership and self-control: financial participation and economic democracy

In a broad sense, theoretical discussion of the scope for workplace democratization pivots around the question of ownership. To what extent do constraints attributable specifically to private and narrowly based ownership make the democratization of work impracticable? I shall not deal directly with State ownership at the systemic level, although the pattern of national ownership is obviously relevant to organizational control.[1] On the other hand, the discussion includes democratic forms of ownership which occupy the no man's land between organizational and national levels. This allows us to address some of the issues raised by the Webbs' dismissal of one type of democratic initiative, workers co-operatives, as 'islands of socialism within a sea of capitalism', unlikely to attain mainland status.

I turn specifically to co-operatives later in this chapter, as one example of democratic ownership. First, I consider briefly the notion of ownership itself, and its relation to the exercise of control. I then look at various approaches to democratizing the economy by changing the distribution of ownership, other than through direct State ownership. The approaches range from wholly individualized forms of financial participation, such as profit-sharing, through producer co-operatives where ownership is (in varying degrees) collective but where the democratization process is internal to the enterprise alone, to proposals for wage-earner funds which aim to extend employee influence more broadly across the economy. Table 8 summarizes the implications of the various approaches for the different aspects of control: internal organization, the economy (at two different levels), and ideology.

Ownership and control

Do owners control? If not, who or what does? The managerialist approach, originated by Berle and Means in the 1930s, sees ownership as a diminishing source of power.[2] The dispersion of share ownership and the technical complexities of running large corporations

Table 8 Ownership and control

| Type of ownership shift | Internal organization | Area of control implicated | | | Ideology | |
| | | Economy | | | | |
		Company level	Macro	Company	National
Profit-sharing	None	Only if pitched at unprecedented level	None	Traditional unitary	Popular capitalism
Co-operatives	Change in authority basis	Egalitarian tendency	Unlikely	Collective unitary, defensive or 'alternative'	Varied: entrepreneurial, traditional socialist, radical
Wage-earner funds	Largely indirect	Potentially strategic	Possible	Pluralist	Corporatist

mean that control of company policy is effectively in the hands of salaried professionals. Individual shareholders simply receive interest on their capital, but are not in a position to participate in corporate decision-making. The constraints of profit maximization are therefore loosened, and managers can—and do—concentrate on other objectives, such as steady company growth. This perceived trend is further taken in some cases to represent a qualitative change in the nature of capitalism, with the disappearance of owner control significantly changing the parameters of industrial decision-making.

There are several lines of opposition to this. Perhaps the crudest is that whether or not such a shift has taken place makes no difference, since market pressures determine company behaviour to such an extent that profit maximization is still obligatory. Variations in managerial perceptions and work-force strengths and orientations are therefore irrelevant. Subtler is the argument that owners and managers may no longer be the same people, but this has little effect on company policy and practice since the two share the same ideology. Although managers may have only a small financial holding in the company in which they are employed, they are nevertheless likely to be members of the small class of private capital-owners, and correspondingly unlikely to take a position which damages the interests of that class.[3] A further line of argument agrees that ownership is becoming more dispersed and in general less closely linked to management. However, the very fact of dispersion means that private shareholders still retain control in most instances, since ownership of a relatively small proportion of shares is sufficient to ensure domination of the vote. There is some disagreement on exactly how big the proportion has to be, but 5 to 10 per cent is the range normally cited.[4]

In part the debate revolves around, on the one hand, the relative importance of the attitudes and behaviour of individuals and, on the other, the structural constraints on their actions. It also covers a variety of conceptions of control, ranging from the highly specific and overt (for example over the appointment of senior management) to the diffuse and subtle. We have covered some of this ground in previous chapters, but the issue is further complicated by two factors. First, there is the emergence of the giant financial institutions, notably insurance companies and pension funds, as dominant actors on the economic stage—indeed, these two are the largest holders of quoted stock, with 46 per cent of the total between them in 1981. In the UK the institutions have until recently intervened very rarely in company management, though there are signs that this is changing. But by their very nature they influence the shape of economic activity.

Moreover their growth has meant that one has to consider not only their role as owners, but also how they themselves are controlled. We do this in Chapter 5.

Secondly, the notion of ownership is in any case not as straightforward as it might appear to most non-legal eyes. It has, for example, been argued that approaches to the relation between ownership and control are often ill-founded because they misunderstand the legal character of the modern joint-stock firm.[5] In layman's terms, Jawaharlal Nehru made the point as follows:

The very idea of private property, which seems to some people one of the fundamental notions of the world, has been an ever-changing one. Shares were property at one time, and so were women and children, the seigneur's right to the bride's first night, roads, temples, ferries, public utilities, air and land. Animals are still property, though legislation has in many countries limited the right of ownership. During wartime there is a continuous infringement of property rights. Property today is becoming more and more intangible.[6]

Bearing in mind, then, that whilst a shift in ownership may be a necessary condition for the democratization of work, the concept of ownership is neither a simple nor a static one, I turn to consider specific ways in which democratization is interpreted directly in terms of a reformed pattern of ownership.

Individual financial participation: profit-sharing

'Financial participation' will not be used to refer to cash hand-outs or other forms of bonus. These can only be properly included under the heading of 'participation' if other forms of surplus distribution are also included—and that would include orthodox wage bargaining. The key feature is whether some modification of ownership is involved. That said, 'profit-sharing' is often used to cover a variety of schemes designed to promote individual share ownership rather than, as its name implies, the distribution of surplus. Given that employee participation in company decision-making did not emerge as a discrete issue until earlier this century, the widespread if often ephemeral incidence of profit-sharing schemes in the nineteenth century gives this form of participation a certain historical precedence. In France, indeed, the primary meaning of 'participation' is profit-sharing, with a Gaullist initiative in 1959 (followed by legislation in 1967) requiring firms with more than 100 employees to give workers shares in the company. In the UK, there are three main categories of individual financial participation other than cash-based schemes.

(Other countries naturally have different systems, the variations normally deriving from particular fiscal arrangements.)

- *Profit-based financial participation.* In essence this resembles a bonus scheme, except that shares are distributed instead of cash. The amount distributed is related to the company's profit, usually as a fixed or variable percentage of total profits. There may be a threshold profit level to be attained before the scheme is triggered. In general, shares must be retained for a certain period, especially if they are to attract the full fiscal benefits; the 1978 Finance Act laid down that the percentage of the capital value which is taxable declines as the period for which they are held increases, so that at the end of ten years' ownership all tax liability ceases. Employees are usually only eligible if they have served a minimum qualifying period with the company. The shares can be distributed immediately to individual employees or held in trust for them during the specified retention period. If the shares are held in trust, not only do the employees not become the owners, they also will not receive the dividends directly—though the trust can decide to distribute revenues earned.

- *Executive share options or incentives.* As the name implies, these schemes are aimed at senior management employees, who have so far been the main beneficiaries of profit-sharing generally. Under an option scheme, a small down payment gives the executive the option to purchase shares in the future, usually at a discount and with favourable loan terms available. Under an incentive scheme, the shares are purchased at the outset, so the benefits start flowing at once. It is worth noting that executives are commonly guaranteed against actual loss, so the shares hardly represent 'risk' capital.

- *Savings-related schemes.* Employees pay in a certain contribution from their earnings over a given period of time in order to acquire a shareholding in their company. They may receive rights and/or benefits from the outset, and following the 1980 Finance Act in the UK this sort of scheme also qualifies for tax advantages.

The objectives of financial participation can be divided into a number of categories, and have rather different significances according to whether they refer to the level of the individual enterprise or to the economy nationally. It is, incidentally, questionable whether the initiators of schemes—employers or legislators—have themselves a clear view of what they expect to accomplish by them.

The simplest rationale for extending financial participation is that everyone should share in the material wealth produced. Sometimes this is given an explicitly redistributive slant, in that workers without capital are given the opportunity to acquire some, though this claim generally appears thin given that most schemes are structured so that higher earners benefit more. A second argument points not to the amount of capital involved, but to the mere fact that employees are encouraged to possess some at all—to the *incidence* of ownership rather than the *distribution* of wealth. In the mid-1970s, less than 4 per cent of all British adults had any direct shareholdings, which is seen as one reason for apathetic attitudes to economic performance. This, the classic 'worker capitalist' argument, can be applied at two levels: nationally in order to influence political thinking in favour of a particular system of property ownership, or at company level in order to foster a unitary spirit amongst employees. Thirdly, whether or not the ideological impact is achieved, the financial incentive may be sufficient to influence their economic behaviour. Fourthly, a company may promote profit-sharing not for its material benefits but specifically as a way of giving itself a corporate identity, reinforcing in its employees a feeling of belonging to a particular body. Fifthly, the fiscal advantages may be such that a company calculates that it would be passing up the opportunity of public subsidy if it did not offer financial participation. This is particularly so if it can persuade its employees that it is incurring the costs itself, and thus trade them off against other possible labour costs.

There is, then, a mixture of material, moral, and ideological reasons for the promotion of financial participation. But the key question is how far financial participation affects power relationships at the workplace. Does ownership of the type envisaged bring with it the opportunity to influence decision-making, or does it weaken employees' ability to advance their own interests?

The evidence is very sparse. The usual imposition of a period over which shares must be retained is a clear indication that the aim is to reward long service. Profit-sharing can therefore be set alongside other quasi-paternalist measures designed to promote company loyalty, or policies favouring an internal labour market with structured career ladders. On the other hand, the fact that benefits start to accrue only at the end of a retention period amounting to several years makes it more difficult for anyone to make the connection between their own behaviour and subsequent rewards, especially in larger organizations, where the impact on profits of the actions of an individual or even a group of workers is infinitesimal.

As one might expect, the United States, with its tradition of livelier individual shareholder interest, has shown more activity in this field, with an estimated 300,000 firms running some form of profit-sharing scheme. Some studies report an impact on employee attitudes, but no connection is established with participation in decision-making. Most recently there has been an upsurge (also partly fiscally induced) of Employee Stock Ownership Plans (ESOPs). Share purchase is operated through a trust, which uses money borrowed from the company and eventually releases the shares to individual employees. There are now several thousand ESOPs. Yet in very few cases are the trusts even formally in a position to exercise voting rights, and the direct impact of the plans on the pattern of control has been wholly marginal.[7]

Share ownership does generally carry with it rights of voting, as well as of attending shareholder meetings and so forth. Yet the rationales outlined above rarely envisage any link between financial participation and shareholder influence. On the whole this is completely realistic. As the original ownership/control debate showed, individual shareholders, especially on the minute scale which generalized financial participation involves, are largely powerless. Only in an indirect sense might it be true that individual financial participation of the kind described above will affect company decision-making: if a growth in the shareholdings of employees leads them to take a more active interest in the company's strategy, and raises their aspirations to participate. Managements introducing profit-sharing schemes are apparently confronted by the familiar dilemma of participation: if the scheme has no impact, it is hardly worth the employer's while; yet the more effective a scheme becomes, the more it poses a threat to established patterns of control.

The answer is, not surprisingly, that profit-sharing is not intended to have any impact on the frontiers of control. Von Thünen, the German originator of profit-sharing schemes, produced complex computations to identify the point at which the wider distribution of share ownership would begin substantially to affect control. The debate over wage-earner funds (pp. 71–5) revolves in part around the pace of the transfer, i.e. the proportion of ownership to be transferred within a given period. But it is an indication of the limited expectations of profit-sharing that future projections rarely deal with the prospect of a transformation of ownership which would have significant control implications.

Finally, economic circumstances have recently produced a crop of management buy-outs. These entail a significant modification in the pattern of ownership, from external to internal owners, and the transition is often engineered by a group of employees acting collectively. As such they provide an appropriate bridge to the discussion of worker co-operatives. But as their name implies, management buy-outs involve only senior employees, and the motivation is normally simply the belief that the organization can be economically viable if reshaped. Even in theory they will not recast employment relationships.

Internal democratization: workers' co-operatives[8]

Co-operatives have already had a long time to prove themselves. Their history has been amply documented from the philanthropic initiatives of Robert Owen through to the paradoxical impetus given by the contemporary collapse of conventional employment.[9] They still form only a minute section of the economy, yet they continue to arouse public interest and encourage the belief that idealism and practical business are not incompatible. The sustained success of the Mondragon set of collectives in the Basque region of Spain has been particularly influential,[10] though the less publicized Italian co-operatives are a more important sector of their national economy. So are co-operatives merely destined to emerge into and recede from prominence without lasting impact? Or are they adding substantially to the deposits of knowledge and pioneering experience of democratic processes?

Although there are a host of different types of co-operative, they adhere more or less faithfully to the following criteria: (i) the establishment is autonomous, (ii) employees are able to become members of the enterprise by nominal holdings of share capital, (iii) the principle of 'one-member-one-vote' prevails, (iv) formal provision exists for direct employee participation at all levels, (v) employees share in profits.[11] The principles which underlie them illustrate the link between capital ownership and control of the workplace. But given that political parties with very different ideologies support co-operatives, both the principles and the link are clearly susceptible to different interpretations—another example of verbal uniformity disguising actual plurality.

The more legalistic approaches concern themselves with whether the establishment conforms to certain constitutional requirements, but exclude consideration of internal patterns of authority and control. We shall simply note that there are two major legal categories of co-operatives, defined under the 1976 Common Ownership Act as common ownership and co-operative enterprises, the former being rather more precisely defined than the latter. They may be registered under the Industrial and Provident Societies Acts, or under the Companies Act as companies limited by guarantee without share capital. They may have a two-tier structure, where the shares are held by a holding company and membership is restricted to members of the trading company. Such variations—and the several subdivisions within each of them—will concern us only in so far as they have particular relevance for the way decisions are taken within co-operatives. The bulk of our attention will be on the degree to which co-operatives represent, actually or potentially, a significant extension of democracy at work. This involves three aspects: the extent to which co-operatives as a whole are genuinely autonomous, i.e. free from outside control; the control which co-operators are able to exercise over their own work; and the extent to which co-operatives act as a dynamic element, opening up ideological and practical 'space' for further democratization.

Autonomy

Formally, co-operatives are autonomous in that they have disposed of external shareholders who can exploit their ownership of capital to influence workplace decision-making. In conventional capitalist companies, shareholders normally exercise this power by divesting themselves of shares rather than by any active intervention. Co-operators aim to avoid the obligation to pay out their surplus in the form of dividends and thus eliminate this negative power.

But formal autonomy may be undermined by broader economic factors. In the first place, the obverse of independence from external shareholders is increased reliance on other external sources of finance. Co-operators traditionally are not in a position to supply substantial sums of capital themselves, and must seek support elsewhere in the form of loans or grants. The loans can be purely commercial, or provided on special terms by sympathetic public or trust bodies. The terms can be without strings, or carry with them certain conditions (such as a change in management, product, or working practices) which effectively restore the power of the outside capital holder. Orthodox lending institutions are likely to exercise close supervision in view of the co-operative's lack of collateral.

Financial constraints on co-operatives are severe. Not only are they cut off from conventional capital sources, usually to an extent which outweighs the support available from sympathetic alternatives, but they also face market problems often more pressing than those confronting conventional firms. Co-operatives born out of failure by definition inherit an unhealthy economic legacy. On top of this, they are likely to find suppliers shortening their period of credit and restrictive in the terms on which they supply their goods, leading rapidly to a cash-flow problem. In some cases, commercial mistrust is exacerbated by ideological hostility towards an alternative form of productive organization. At the other end of the business, co-operators find themselves in difficulties over pricing and selling policies: inexperience, the immediate need for work, or an antipathy towards profit-seeking may lead them to conclude economically unrealistic contracts.

Apart from its direct links with financiers, suppliers, and customers, a co-operative's autonomy depends more broadly on its position within the market and within the national or international division of labour. Table 9 shows that co-operatives tend to be concentrated in particular sectors, typically, though not exclusively, in areas associated with alternative life-styles, such as wholefood or craft shops. In part this is due to the low capital requirements of such activities. Even those in the more traditional industrial sectors tend to be at the bottom end of the market, carrying out assembly, repair, and maintenance work. Whether or not it is attributable specifically to the familiar bugbear of the multinational company, as has been suggested,[12] the precarious market position of many co-operatives is certainly enough to remind us how they bob about in the backwash of larger enterprises.

However, co-operatives generally suffer if they attempt to insulate themselves from the wider economy. This restricts their trading outlets and scope. More importantly, it deprives them of essential feedback. The notion of the market-place as providing 'discipline' is anathema to many co-operators, yet attempts to reject it wholesale (and other standard commercial indicators with it) often mean that organizational practice and trading policies go badly awry.[13] Such indicators need not be allowed to rule, yet they can rarely be ignored.

The State can help with direct measures to enlarge the scope for autonomy and survival. The 1976 Common Ownership Act facilitated the growth of co-operatives by providing loan facilities, and two years later the Co-operative Development Agency was established to give organizational assistance. Local agencies have also been set up. In 1980, about one-third of the existing co-operatives had received some form of help from the State.

Table 9 A breakdown of the number of worker co-operatives by industrial sector in 1980 and 1982

Trading activities	1980		1982	
	No. of co-ops	Percentage of total	No. of co-ops	Percentage of total
1. Advisory, consultative, and educational (including computer software, insurance, language schools)	21	6.4	33	6.6
2. Building, house renovations, and house decorations; cleaning; waste recycling	33	10.0	69	13.8
3. Crafts, carpentry, furniture-making and joinery	19	5.8	40	8.0
4. Engineering electronics, chemicals	26	7.9	41	8.2
5. Footwear, clothing, and textile manufacture	19	5.8	32	6.4
6. Printing and publishing	61	18.5	75	15.0
7. Provision and hire of transport; bicycle and motor vehicle repairs	11	3.3	13	2.6
8. Record, film, and music making; theatre (including actors' agencies)	28	8.5	46	9.2
9. Retail, distributive, catering, and food processing	112	33.9	151	30.4
Total:	330		500	
Total no. of co-ops (adjusted to take account of those with more than one trading activity)	304		483	

Source: C. Cornforth, 'Some Factors Affecting the Success or Failure of Worker Co-operatives: A Review of Empirical Evidence in the UK', *Economic and Industrial Democracy* 4:2 (1983), 167.

Autonomy of a sort may be secured through self-exploitation. Survival depends on the payment of wages below the going rate. Fear of this is the major source of union hostility to co-operatives, or at least nullifies the natural sympathy towards a collective enterprise. By embodying cheap labour, co-operatives not only themselves do not conform to union practice, but also provide some leverage, however flimsy, for employers to keep down local wage rates. How far this actually occurs is unproven, but it has historically influenced the attitudes of many in the labour movement.

However, the notion of exploitation needs further scrutiny. Wages are compensation for surrendering one's labour power, but co-operators do not surrender their own labour power to others. Wages are not the sole measure of their reward, and surplus value is not removed from their control. Other, non-material benefits which co-operators receive vary and may well be uncertain: job security, for example, is a motivating goal which may not be achieved in the long term. Co-operatives raise qualitative questions of relative values, which make verdicts on them difficult, even with substantial historical evidence. Orthodox accountancy and economic evaluation techniques are simply inadequate for the purpose.

Internal democracy

Co-operatives explicitly espouse the one-member-one-vote principle, though rarely in pure form—i.e. there are usually some workers employed on a conventional non-membership basis. Whilst formally this ensures some degree of direct participation, it tells us little about the actual process of decision-making. In a general sense, co-operatives are likely to evince a stronger commitment to participation than the average enterprise. Even where they are firmly oriented to a market economy, the ownership structure militates to some extent against a traditional authority structure. However, there will be obvious variations. The commitment to democracy may be interpreted in purely formal terms. Between 1890 and 1970 producer co-operatives on the whole maintained or even increased the level of worker representation within management committees, and in that sense more and more societies became self-governing. However, when the extent to which the industrial relations reality corresponds to formal structures is examined, the picture is more uncertain.[14] We shall look at two interrelated aspects: the role of management and the division of labour.

In a conventional firm, management is responsible to the shareholders. Shareholders can vote with their hands to remove management, or with their feet by taking their capital elsewhere. Formally, there is no responsibility towards the employees. Again formally, the constitution of co-operatives solves this problem. Management is made responsible to the work-force, with no external shareholders to influence it. Management therefore derives its authority not from external sources but from its contract with the work-force. The practicability of this has been doubted,[15] but at a conceptual level confusion persists about the place of management within co-operatives. Association of the term with its capitalist form leads to a wholesale rejection of the need for managers of any kind. 'Management' is thrown out along with 'managers', functions and skills being conflated with a particular category of employees.

Yet management—whether people or function—is not a permanently defined phenomenon. In its human form, this is obvious: individual managers come and go in the normal course of business life, and management as a group may be radically transformed by a takeover or by a democratic upheaval. Confusion arises when the function is regarded—usually implicitly—as a fixed entity, to be taken or left. Obviously several elements go to make up the total management function, and these are conventionally broken down into finance, production, personnel, sales, and so forth. Two questions arise: how is the division of managerial functions arrived at, and who is to discharge them?

In both cases, the answers may involve a mix of old and new. That is, it is unlikely that all the previous skills regarded as necessary for the management of the firm can be totally discarded under a new system; it is also possible that people who filled managerial posts in conventional enterprise structures could do the same within a co-operatives. The problem is to decide how much of their experience and skills remains valid.[16]

The building guilds, a network of co-operatives set up in the early 1920s, were initially very successful in developing their work and reviving employment in the building industry. But a lack of managerial skills, combined with the withdrawal of government financial assistance, brought them crashing down. More recently, Eccles's account of KME is, despite his sympathy for the enterprise and for the two conveners who led the co-operative, forthrightly critical: 'The leaders were never interested in factual analyses, and their antipathy towards normal management systems, which was shared by many co-operators, made them rotten at running the business . . . This might not have mattered if the leaders had instead created a charter for the professional managers so that effective management of the business could occur; but they didn't. They simultaneously rejected the management role for themselves and refused to give it to the managers.'[17] The failure of enterprise management, allowing for the co-operative's difficult circumstances, is documented: poor product development, marketing, pricing policy and so forth. Even industrial relations were patchy, as the conveners struggled to come to grips with their dual role. Eccles's analysis provides many practical lessons. Equally interesting, however, is the fact that he never treats the concept of 'management' as at all problematic. The impression is given that there is one correct way to manage a business, and that is a matter for professionals. Yet for co-operatives (as indeed for all democratic ventures) there is a constant challenge to redefine the concept of management, to bring it under control instead of accepting it as externally derived from more or less alien principles.

For example, given that management in a conventional firm has a disciplinary as well as a co-ordinating function, how is this to be discharged in a co-operative? 'Self-control' implies just that: the exercise of control over oneself, as well as the freedom from control by others. But part of the (collective) self may fail to do this. Naturally, neither the disciplinary code nor the sanctions need be the same as within an orthodox managerial structure, but they demand consideration.[18] The problem of discipline within democracy is not unique to co-operatives, but it provides a good if awkward example of the need to reconsider both the allocation and the content of managerial functions within the overall division of labour.

The rejection of professional management is part of a more general ambivalence within the co-operative movement towards the division of labour. Co-operation could be interpreted as collaborating with one's fellows literally in doing the same work, not merely in working alongside them. But the extent to which specialization—and in particular the idea of specialized management roles—can be discouraged varies greatly. Job rotation is often tried and sometimes abandoned. Thornley found that in every co-operative with over twenty members there was a degree of task specialization, though whether this was a major source of dissatisfaction is uncertain. It cannot be a question of whether or not there is division of labour (horizontal or vertical), but of its extent and the way in which it is decided upon.

It has been suggested (by the Webbs amongst others) that co-operatives inherently tend to move away from a democratic structure back to an orthodox management system; similarly that they will revert to a conventional division of labour. Certainly they are under major constraints if they wish to compete in the market-place, as we discussed in the previous section. But crude versions of such organizational and technical determinism are merely the obverse of the naïve view that no managerial function or division of labour at all is necessary. The evidence on 'degeneration' is not at all conclusive. Naturally the organization's form will change over time, but the process is unlikely to be simple.

It is true that co-operators have often faced hard choices between increasing productive efficiency and maintaining co-operative principles. But in so far as these are incompatible, there need be no greater degree of conflict than that which faces capitalist firms which also have multiple objectives. The very fact that co-operators have constructed such a choice for themselves marks them off favourably from many other workers.

Models of democratic experience

From the start there has been an integral link between co-operatives and learning. The Rochdale Pioneers included provision for the education of members in co-operative principles in their original manifesto (along with such others as religious neutrality and selling only unadulterated goods). Today the co-operative movement still has an elaborate system of formal education, with its own institutions and curricula. But its significant educational role lies more in the experience acquired by active participants on the one hand, and the presentation to the public of a model of democratic endeavour on the other.

It is here that the differences between the various political conceptions of co-operation emerge most sharply. At one end, there is the hope that co-operatives will constitute a thriving *small business* sector. Entrepreneurial zeal is generated by the feeling of working for themselves and not for an external shareholder. Clearly, this has much in common with the rationale for profit-sharing: enhanced sensitivity to market factors and a stress on the beneficial effects of determined self-interest. The internal organization of the enterprise and its social character are of interest only in so far as they affect economic performance.

Alternative describes those co-operatives whose members reject contemporary life-styles. Rejection may be restricted to dietary issues (though even here there is a wide variation, from the promotion of wholemeal bread for reasons of physical health to the religiously motivated exclusion of animal-derived products), or it may be more fundamentally related to the ethos of modern society. Although some proselytizing may be involved, the focus of the co-operators is on controlling their own lives in accordance with their own principles. The space created is their own.

Thirdly, *defensive* co-operators are formed to protect employment in the face of threatened closure. These generally have no particular positive ideology, though there is often a strong current of resentment against the forces which have provoked the formation of the co-operative. Economic circumstances mean that there is little room or time for the pursuit of principles; on the other hand the collective spirit created by the co-operative's foundation may be deemed essential for its survival, not to be sacrificed for some marginal economic gain. The three so-called Benn co-operatives—KME, Scottish Daily News, and Meriden—all fall under this heading. Named after the then Secretary of State for Industry, their experience illustrates both the impact of governmental activity and the constraints on it: a determined and influential politician secured resources, and a very high profile, for the co-operatives, but the timing was arguably all awry and the initiative was anyway undermined, politically by the lack of whole-hearted State commitment and organizationally by the problems referred to earlier. There are, however, signs that some of these lessons have been digested.

Fourthly, *traditional* co-operatives have their roots in nineteenth-century socialism, and their political complexion reflects their origins. It envisages industrial society shifting to more democratic and socially responsible forms of governance, but is slow to absorb the implications of trends in modern capitalism. Part of the weight which co-operatives carry—disproportionate to their economic significance —derives from the longevity of this tradition and the experience it affords. Their space is historical.

Finally there are co-operatives whose members are strongly motivated by *radical* ideas, tying co-operatives in as one element of a broader socialist transformation. Co-operatives not only clear their own space, but collaborate with other political movements in order to make space for all. Active alliance with trade unions and socialist parties is an integral part of their programme. They aim to drain off the capitalist sea so that Beatrice Webb's islands become an archipelago or even a continental land mass.

Evaluations of the co-operative experience must therefore capture a number of dimensions.[19] The variety of co-operative forms, though less than those of participation generally, still defies generalization. It is true that co-operatives operate in an economic environment which constrains their freedom of organization. But it is only a constraint, not a total determinant. Thus co-operatives add a further dimension of variability to our picture of the decision-making process; they expand the range of alternatives.

Co-operatives also illustrate how tension and conflict are not banished by democratic forms—or, for that matter, by democratic substance. They still have to make choices between the short-term and the long-term future, between their own interests and those of the world outside, between their own diverse interests. Allocative and distributive issues, and even personal scores, still have to be settled. Perhaps the most significant feature of co-operatives is that they claim the formal right and the formal responsibility to confront those issues explicitly.

Collective financial participation: wage-earner funds

By their very nature, co-operatives are constrained in the extent to which they affect the distribution of power in the economic and social system. The exercise of external ownership rights conflicts directly with the principle that only working members should have voting powers. Thus their contribution to the process of democratization is constituted mainly by their own internal character; the effect on others is limited to the power of their example.

Other schemes exist which do not simply propose to transfer ownership into public hands and yet which aim to extend democratization beyond the confines of a single organization into the broader economy. In that sense, they conform more fully than previous initiatives to the notion of 'economic democracy' discussed in the Introduction. The ideas under review here have been implemented only in one country, and too recently there to be evaluated. However, they have already had a broader theoretical and political impact than this might suggest, filling at least part of the gap between levels of State and enterprise control.

Proposals for collective financial participation are more commonly termed employee or wage-earner funds, distinguishing them from individual profit-sharing schemes from which they have a different rationale and structure. They are characterized by one or more of the following features: emphasis on equitable ownership of capital as much (or more than) the distribution of benefits flowing from it; concern with the balance between capital accumulation and income levels; concern with the social and economic use to which capital is put; the desire to democratize decision-making over capital and at the workplace. Collective ownership makes the simultaneous attainment of these goals possible, in theory at least, in a way that profit-sharing schemes geared to individual ownership cannot.

Proposals for employee funds are of far more recent date than profit-sharing, though it is several decades since G. D. H. Cole, outlining the case against the latter, made the distinction we have adopted between collective and individual forms of financial participation.[20] The chief architect of collective funds has been Rudolf Meidner, an economist working for the Swedish manual trade union confederation, LO. His original objective was to reconcile three aims: (1) the encouragement of leading dynamic sectors in the Swedish economy; (2) the preservation of LO's solidaristic wage policy, which opposed large wage differentials arising simply from the fact that workers happen to be located in more and less profitable industries; (3) the bringing of capital under more democratic control. (1) and (2) combined would lead to a massive and inequitable concentration of private wealth, as the surpluses permitted in profitable industries by worker self-restraint (in line with solidaristic policy) would simply accrue to shareholders. Meidner's idea was that a proportion of company profits above a certain level would be paid into a workers' fund, the payments to be made directly in the form of shares, or in cash which the funds would use to buy shares on the stock exchange. The companies' capital base would thus be preserved, without causing an inequitable concentration of private wealth. Income from the shareholdings would be used to buy further shares and to support educational activities of benefit to employees.[21]

Considerably modified, the proposals reached the statute-book in 1983. In its legislated form the system consists of five separate employee investment funds. Each will have an income of about 2bn. Swedish kronor annually, derived from a 20 per cent levy on profits above a certain level and a 0.2 per cent payroll levy. (Some firms, particularly smaller ones, will be exempt.) Interestingly, in view of the discussion which follows in Chapter 5, the funds will now be linked in to the Swedish supplementary pensions system, which will receive the returns from their investment activities. The funds are expected to make a real annual return of 3 per cent, but to have a conscious orientation to the long term. The objectives of the system are now described as follows: to *reduce* conflict over the distribution of income, wage drift, and inflation; to *increase* the availability of risk capital; and to *give workers* direct responsibility for the use of risk capital, a share of future profits, and a greater measure of influence in the enterprise.

The management board of each fund, first appointed in March 1984, consists of nine members, appointed by the government. At least five of these are 'to represent the interests of the employees'; normally, but not necessarily, this will mean people active in trade unions. At this level, therefore, the system entails majority representation on boards governing capital which is projected to amount to about 5 per cent of all listed shares in Sweden by 1990. No one fund may hold more than 8 per cent of the voting shares of a given company; the hypothetical limit of the five funds' holding in a single company, when added to that of the Pension Fund board which deals in shares (10 per cent), is thus half of the voting rights. The funds are expected to be able to influence company policy, but not to dominate it outright.

Local influence is to be secured by the requirement that each board should have a regional affiliation, though the country will not be formally carved up. But there is a further significant level at which the system promotes participation. If the local union organization so requests, the funds must transfer to it half of the voting rights conferred by their shareholdings. Workers already have the right to board-level representation as employees, following the co-determination legislation (MBL), of 1976; to this may now be added the right of representation as shareholders. So there is a conscious attempt to promote the integration of participation at several levels and through a number of instruments concurrently.

It is far too early to judge the impact of this initiative on economic performance, capital control, or the distribution of power at the workplace. The fundamental debate concerns the nature of ownership and property rights. Given its position—unchallenged until recently—as the pioneer of social democracy within capitalist countries, it is perhaps remarkable that Sweden has one of the lowest proportions of State ownership, with under 10 per cent of the means of production in State hands. Social control has been sought through other means, such as highly progressive fiscal and social policies. The tensions set up by the concentration of capital (especially within a small country heavily dependent on exports from a limited number of industries) have forced the issue of ownership to the fore. But the rationale for wage-earner funds has always given a prominent place to the objective of increasing employee control at the workplace. It is precisely the explicit establishment of this link between ownership and control which makes the scheme significant for our purposes.

The proposals naturally provoked vociferous opposition from the representatives of capital, and contain a number of foreseeable problems. Participation by public employees, especially in the non-trading sector, is problematic. The reaction of foreign capital, especially that located in subsidiaries of foreign-owned multinationals, may threaten stability. The internal and external accountability of union representatives will come under severe scrutiny. How far the shop-floor will perceive themselves as more effectively involved is a matter for particular speculation, but a major premium will be placed on the quality of communication between representatives and their constituents.

These problems are common to many other initiatives towards democracy at work. One further difficulty is peculiarly relevant to these proposals: the acute complexity of the structure, with its multiple funds and overlapping systems of representation. Sweden's smallness, relative homogeneity, degree of centralization, and general proficiency in social management make it easier to envisage such a structure working there than almost anywhere else.

The system could not, for example, be easily transposed to the UK with its far more diverse and decentralized union structure. Nevertheless, employee funds are not a Swedish peculiarity.[22] Similar proposals have been seriously considered in Denmark, though in a less thoroughgoing collectivist form, as workers would be able to withdraw their stakes after a given period. Other countries which have addressed themselves to the question of employee influence on collective capital formation include the Netherlands and Austria, but the economic recession seems to have reduced much of the impetus behind such ideas. In Britain, the Labour party published a Green Paper in 1973 which took up the idea of employee funds in explicit opposition to profit-sharing.[23] It proposed that companies should make over 1 per cent of their equity shares annually to a collective fund in which both public—and private-sector workers would participate, with the right at the end of seven years to cash a proportion of their entitlements each year. The TUC would have a majority in the fund's management body. Both the TUC and the Labour party now look more to occupational pension funds as a form of collective capital over which employee influence and democratic control can be achieved. But the idea of collective employee funds cannot be ruled out as a concrete political option, especially given continuing concern with the distribution of wealth, capital accumulation, incomes policy, investment strategy, and the accountability of capital. Its contribution to the democratization process, however, may come to be seen as much in having laid the basis for a reconsideration of the links between ownership and control as in putting forward a specific system of financial participation.

Conclusion

We have reviewed various initiatives to change the distribution of ownership. Profit-sharing schemes may offer material benefits to individuals as part of the employee remuneration package and are essentially a matter of the distribution of surplus. As such they are subject to the same type of conflict as are conventional wages and other fringe benefits. They have little significance for the patterns of control. Co-operatives are based on a degree of collectivism and a breaking of the link between external ownership and control. The conduct of worker-owners is subject to external constraints, but they have been able to develop a range of alternative forms of organization and practice. Collective employee funds represent a more fundamental challenge to existing patterns of control. If they achieve substantial form, they will be confronted by the problems of extended ownership. In particular, the collective ethos which underpins them will be tested by the dilemmas of planning at different economic levels, the reconciliation of long- and short-term goals, the interests of diverse groups of workers, and workers' aspirations for control of their own funds.

5 Occupational welfare and capital control: participation in the management of pension schemes

In this chapter and the following one, we turn to two specific areas of corporate decision-making in which there have been significant moves towards greater participation in the last decade. Chapter 6 deals with health and safety; here we look at the management of occupational pension schemes.[1]

We noted in Chapter 4 the emergence of financial institutions as major actors on the economic scene, with pension funds prominent amongst these. The funds now own assets which total about £140bn. ($1,000bn. in the US). Their shareholdings alone amount to £35bn. (up from £7.5bn. in 1975). But it is not only the size of the funds which makes pension schemes important. They are an increasingly significant component of the employment relationship. Wages form only a part of labour's reward; many of the benefits which used to be called 'fringe' are now an integral part of remuneration, and an occupational pension is one of the most prominent.

Worker participation in pensions decision-making therefore has two dimensions. First, it involves representatives in the shaping and implementation of a system of occupational welfare, in which benefits are provided on the basis of a person's status as an employee, rather than as a citizen. Participation here, whether or not it takes the form of collective bargaining, allows us to consider in a specific and practical context some of the arguments about incorporation, the notion that participation serves to integrate workers and their representatives into a given system without disturbing underlying inequalities of power. Secondly there is the control of capital via employee representation on the boards of trustees which are formally responsible for the pension schemes' assets (the funds). Contemporary experience allows us to contrast the potential for economic democracy with the limited influence which this form of representation has so far exercised on the direction of capital, and to speculate briefly on future directions.

The growth of participation

The State provides a basic level of support for retired people, but this has increasingly been supplemented by an elaborate system of occupational pensions, based on contributions by employer and employee (or employer only) and buttressed by fiscal subsidy. Occupational pensions have existed for decades, but the system was set on a firm footing only in the 1970s, with the Social Security Acts of 1973 and 1975.[2] Occupational pension schemes now have 11,000,000 members, who enjoy an annual tax subsidy which may be as high as £5 bn.

Historically, pensions (and from now on we shall be referring to occupational pensions only) were seen as *ex gratia* payments, a benevolent gesture normally afforded as reward for long and faithful service. In the private sector, a pension was a classic mark of paternalism. It was granted at the employer's discretion, the amount being also a matter of wholly unilateral decision.[3] Pensions encouraged loyalty, and the threat of their withdrawal was a potent weapon in the hands of employers.

Gradually, however, pensions have come to be seen as deferred pay. If employers were not making direct provision for the pensions of their employees they would have to increase wages by an equivalent amount to allow employees to make their own provision. As a consequence of this transition from paternalism, pensions are becoming a more regular feature of negotiations between unions and employers. There may be a noticeable time-lag between the recognition of pensions as deferred pay and their inclusion as a regular negotiable item (unlike the US, where pensions are mandatorily subject to negotiation). But the trend constitutes a substantial example of the extension of collective bargaining, a frontier of control shifted to bring another segment of corporate policy under some degree of joint decision-making. Employer attitudes towards this are mixed: some have resisted the expansion of negotiation, but others have positively encouraged the inclusion of pensions in collective bargaining, since this makes the trade-off between wages now and higher pensions in the future quite explicit.[4]

However, more spectacular has been the growth of non-bargaining modes of participation, especially on the trustee boards which are formally responsible for managing the funds. There are nearly 100,000 pension schemes, and most of the smaller ones simply hand over their money to an insurance company. Larger schemes, however, are governed by boards of trustees, and the development of employee representation at this level has been both substantial and rapid. About half of these larger schemes have some degree of representation, the most common form being parity with management appointees. In other words, it is not at all uncommon for the bodies with formal powers over very large chunks of capital to have 50 per cent employee representation. This has occurred, usually over the last six to eight years, with remarkable calmness if one recalls the furore surrounding the Bullock Report's proposals for equal numbers of employee and management representatives on company boards. Later on we shall explain this by reference to the role of trustees and the limited impact of employee representation. Here we deal with the reasons for the upsurge in participation.

First is the shift in the conception of *ownership* in relation to pensions contributions. The acceptance of pensions as deferred pay leads to the conclusion that members should have a right to participate in the management of the money—though the concept of ownership remains blurred, as I discuss below. Secondly, there is the *functional* reason: as the schemes have grown, so management has sought to enlist the help of representatives in their running, especially in the communication function. Third is the threat of *legislation*. In 1976 the Labour government published a White Paper proposing to make parity representation on trustee boards mandatory and based on trade unions.[5] The immediate upsurge of participation initiatives which followed may still be seen as voluntary, but the role of the law cannot be ignored. Fourthly, the *economic growth* of the funds gave them a higher profile and generated a growing concern about their accountability, both to their members and to the public as a whole. Finally, *social* trends towards earlier retirement, accentuated by redundancies and compulsory retirements, prompted a wider interest in how the transition out of work is to be managed.

These reasons are, in varying degrees, specific to the issue of participation in the management of pension schemes. But they can be related to our earlier, more general outline of the sources of power (Chapter 2), for instance concerning the role of legislation. Their strengths can also be compared with the diverse pressures which have given rise to other initiatives, such as the proposals for board-level representation which are discussed in Chapter 8.

Incorporation and excorporation

Occupational welfare can be seen as 'divisive between those in paid employment and the non-employed, between those in covered employment and those who work beside them in non-covered jobs, between the well-covered in the public sector and the badly covered in the private sector, between full-time and part-time workers and between women and men'.[6] Others see it as a significant material advance in changing the distribution of surplus and obliging enterprises to assume some degree of social responsibility. I shall not attempt to review the overall merits of occupational welfare. But employee participation in its management illustrates how participation can accentuate cleavages within the work-force and exacerbate the problems of particular groups already at a relative disadvantage. It also illustrates the problems of bringing together into one framework calculations of the interests of diverse sets of workers.

One strong and common criticism of participation is that it serves as a device to incorporate labour, ideologically or pragmatically. Both employees and their representatives may be incorporated into a general social ethos or into the practices of a particular organization, either or both of which may be seen as reprehensible. The process may also take the cruder form of corruption, the buying off of representatives with material or status offerings. The notion of incorporation, it should be noted, is time-dependent: the argument often turns out to revolve around whether a short-term 'apparent' gain will be paid for in the longer run (or a short-term loss compensated for later).

Two groups are usually seen as liable to incorporation: the work-force as a whole, who are led to act against their own interests, and their representatives, who are induced to betray, knowingly or not, the interests of their constituents. There is, however, a third form of incorporation, where one segment of the work-force neither betrays its own interests nor is sold short by its representatives but achieves a measure of control over its own circumstances at the expense (direct or indirect) of some other segments.[7] To rephrase a well-known dictum, management re-establishes control by sharing it with some at the expense of others. In other words, they *incorporate* some by *excorporating* others, recouping the loss of power to the former by the enhanced control gained over those excluded from the participative process. (The game need not, of course, be zero-sum.) The picture which develops is of a core labour force, relatively secure and also with some measure of participative rights, surrounded by a penumbra of peripheral workers, with few rights and little scope for changing the situation. This has been drawn as general scenario for the future of industrial relations.[8]

The incidence of participation can itself act as a polarizing force by disenfranchising sectors of the work-force.[9] But differing *degrees* of participation can also reinforce polarization. It is certainly the case that qualified and higher-level personnel participate more actively. Whether in doing so they also directly exploit their fellow workers is less clear. West German works councils have been shown to favour the interests of native German, skilled males at the expense of peripheral groups, with immigrant workers being especially excluded from the benefits of codetermination.[10] Financial participation schemes of the sort we discussed in Chapter 4 may induce in the beneficiaries a desire to keep the scheme as exclusive as possible in order to maximize their own benefits. And one charge levelled against co-operators—usually in the theoretical literature but with some empirical support—is that they will tend to refuse to expand employment as this would dilute their own advantages.[11]

It is clear, however, that there is no single core of incorporated workers, but a series of intersecting spheres; some spheres, though of different size, have the same centre, but the centre of one sphere may well be at the periphery of another. A worker will often be a core member from one point of view, peripheral from another—for example, white, full-time, and male, but unskilled. There is therefore no single process of polarization. The pattern is 'polychotomous' not dichotomous, though some of the fissures are naturally wider than others, and they widen, steadily or discontinuously, at different rates.

Participation in the negotiation or management of pension schemes has a dual effect. It is incorporative in a narrow and a broad sense. The involvement of representatives legitimates the pension scheme in the eyes of its members and the system in the eyes of the public at large. More broadly, the combination of material benefit and a measure of social or psychological satisfaction at participating may disguise more fundamental inequalities of wealth and power. This is, it should be noted, true for negotiation as well as other forms of participation. (Indeed in a very general sense the entire system of negotiation—even basic wage bargaining—can be seen as incorporative, in so far as it legitimates the rights of capital to a share in the surplus created and endows labour's challenge with an economistic and not a political character.)

Secondly, participation may have an 'excorporative' impact, leading directly to the exclusion of certain groups or the inequitable treatment of the interests of some members. Rules governing eligibility for a pension scheme are defined by negotiation or by the trustees. In either case, those involved may act so as to define the rules tightly and endow only a restricted group with entitlements, for instance by excluding part-time workers (who are almost all women) or by setting a long qualifying period. Even for those who are already members, participation may serve their interests unequally. Trustees are, it is true, legally obliged to act in the best interests of all beneficiaries, and not on behalf of particular groups. The evidence is that they do this to the best of their abilities. Decision-making within the trustee board is highly consensual. Nevertheless, there are conflicts of interests, though they usually remain covert. Two examples will suffice: pensions in payment (i.e. to those who have already retired) may be increased, but only at the expense of those currently paying in; and those who stay with a single employer tend to benefit substantially at the expense of the 'early leaver' who changes jobs.

The case for democracy rests in part on the assumption that effective representation of genuine interests is necessary for a fair distribution of rewards. The problems of defining interests and fairness are particularly salient in the case of pensions. The trade-off between cash in hand and future benefits, the complexity of professional calculations and the incommensurability of the claims of different groups: all these make it extremely difficult to arrive at just decisions.

In short, participation in the administration of pension schemes exemplifies a number of issues of wider application. It may entail the incorporation of employee representatives into a system which contains and creates structural inequalities, and the concurrent exclusion of peripheral groups from material benefits and democratic rights. Arguably, however, such a position lacks a sense of dynamic. Whilst participation may initially favour only privileged groups, both materially and in terms of decision-making power, it has already eroded employers' unilateral powers over pensions and in the longer term it will help to disseminate both the material benefit and the right to participation more broadly. Involvement can also be seen as a way of building up practical experience in administering an important field of welfare and democratic rights. The issues illustrate how conflicts of interest exist even within a process which the participants themselves regard as integrative and consensual, and that participation, however extensive, does not dissolve such conflicts.

Employee trustees and the control of capital

Trustees have a number of functions. Indeed, their role varies widely, reflecting the fact that the trust system evolved to cope with individual patrimonies, not the huge institutionalized property system that it covers today. Pension fund trustees may control the flow of information concerning the fund, exercise discretionary powers, supervise the application of the trust's rules, appoint the fund's managers and advisers, and monitor its financial performance. But their most significant responsibility is ensuring that the scheme's assets are properly handled, and it is with the impact of participation on the control of pension fund capital that this section is concerned. This allows us to explore further the complex relationship between ownership and control discussed in the previous chapter. Moreover, examination of experience to date reveals a number of constraints on the process of democratization which have a wider application.

Pension funds are now the largest single holders of quoted shares, with 29 per cent of the total in 1983 (up from 17 per cent in 1975). The largest of them are worth over £1bn. each and their gross annual revenues amount to over £10bn. They are by any standards economic giants, and their behaviour is a significant factor influencing financial trends and the terms on which companies have access to capital. The acceptance of the deferred pay principle and the high incidence of participation at trustee level may seem to suffice for the democratization of both ownership and control.[12] But on the empirical evidence available so far, employee trustees appear to exercise little effective control over the capital in their charge. Both they and pensions managers agree that whilst they have had a noticeable impact in some areas, notably the dissemination of information, their contribution to the key activity of investment policy has been minimal.[13]

If pensions are deferred pay, are not employees owners of the funds? After all, no one challenges the ownership of wages. In the first place, however, there is a major temporal disjunction—as much as 40 or more years—between the payment of contributions and the taking up of pension rights. Secondly there is a clear feeling—though with no backing in law or logic—that there is a difference between contributory and non-contributory systems, such that the deferred pay principle is weaker where the employee makes no direct payment. Thirdly, when a scheme is wound up, normally on the occasion of bankruptcy, it is the employer who receives whatever surplus remains after other claims have been met. Surplus in the fund is not automatically assumed to belong to the members. Finally, ownership does not bring with it full rights of disposition. Although individuals may be able to convert some of their pension rights into a lump sum payment, they cannot withdraw their entitlements at their own discretion. In short, the notion of ownership is not clear-cut in relation to the funds (which incidentally makes the ownership of public companies doubly problematic).

Legal ownership therefore is not a secure foundation on which control of the funds can be based. There is a second legal dimension which bears on the issue. Trust law, vague though it is, imposes on trustees a general obligation to act in the best interests of all beneficiaries. This in principle prevents a trustee from favouring one group rather than another, but also from using the funds to further any objectives other than the interests of members. For example, trustees would be in dereliction of their duty if they decided to invest the funds in a project designed only to reinforce national prestige in foreign countries, such as the construction of a military runway—unless it were estimated that the members would ultimately benefit by the increased trade which this might bring. But who is to decide what constitutes the 'best interests'? Hitherto it has been assumed—implicitly—that these could be defined solely in terms of the imme-diate financial returns to investments made. Trustees are legally safeguarded if they follow the advice of professional advisers on finance—and conversely they expose themselves to charges of break-ing their obligation if they unreasonably ignored such advice. How-ever, there is rarely, if ever, any single, demonstrably optimal approach to investment. Even retrospectively and using the most conventional criteria the performance of the funds can be assessed in various ways which produce different answers as to how well they have done. Moreover, the funds' collective size means that willy-nilly they affect the pattern of national economic growth, which in turn affects their members' interests: a stagnant economy means lower pensions for all, as well as less and lower-paid employment.[14]

The problem is conventionally formulated as conflict between economic (revenue-earning) and social (for example employment-creating) objectives. But this is a false antithesis: it is the *time-spans* over which results are judged that are at issue, as well as the *criteria* on which such judgements are made. In this, the apparently arcane topic of the legal obligations of pensions trustees turns out to encapsulate broader questions about participation and the quality of organizational decision-making: what is the range of criteria on which decisions are to be based and over what periods of time?

We cannot conclude even this brief survey of the control implica-tions of legal dispositions without considering their psychological impact. On the one hand, whether or not members do legally own the fund, the growing conviction of their rights as deferred wage-earners gives confidence to claims for substantive participation. On the other hand, awareness of the vagaries of trust law has an inhibiting effect on the desire and capacity to exploit the control opportunities afforded by participation, encouraging passive reliance on professional advisers. Given the importance of confidence for the effectiveness of participation, such factors are highly relevant.

We have seen so far how ambiguous the law is as a source of power for representatives involved in the allocation of pension fund capital. We can now turn briefly to some of the other sources of power listed in Chapter 2: authority, expertise, ideology, and finance. Consideration of these in combination serves to explain the minimal impact which employee representatives have had on the disposition of capital.

There is to a certain extent a division of labour, and authority, amongst participants. Thus the employee representatives are expected to contribute substantially on topics where direct shop-floor reactions can be anticipated. The authority that they carry when advising on how to communicate with scheme members may vanish if they seek to intervene on a matter of strategic financial significance. Conversely, management-appointed trustees bring with them some of the authority of their occupational positions, which is more likely to relate to financial questions. Although this division of authority is not formally sanctioned, it shapes the pattern of decision-making in practice and is widely accepted by the participants. However, the type of expertise which partly endows management with their authority in the organization is not necessarily applicable to decision-making on pension fund capital. Thus the technical justification for their participation may be weaker than is commonly supposed. The real weight of expertise-based power lies with the professional advisers directly involved in pension fund management, whether they are internal (i.e. employees of the organization) or external, drawn from financial institutions such as merchant banks.[15]

In relation to the fund's investment policy, the chief forms of expertise are those of the actuary, the stockbroker, and the banker. The actuary calculates the projected liabilities of the fund and compares it with its current assets. The calculations are highly complex, and the techniques are not such as could be grasped quickly by anyone. Nevertheless the image of a wholly objective set of purely technical operations does not stand up to scrutiny. The calculations are not only subject to error in the inevitable sense that trends and events occur which are beyond their control: mortality and morbidity rates change, and economic circumstances such as inflation rates or stock market earnings veer drastically in one direction or another. They are also based on assumptions, for instance on future earnings, which the actuary can and does change, sometimes after discussions with the employer, and which embody expectations and values which cannot be said to be constants of mathematical neutrality. These may not be made explicit at all. Where they are, it is often difficult for employee representatives to scrutinize them effectively.

The other sources of professional advice can be similarly characterized. There is invariably a mixture of technical assessment and computation with assumptions which may or may not be made explicit and which critically shape the options presented to those who formally constitute the decision-making body. The degree of expertise embodied in this is inevitably a matter of personal judgement. Trustees are often presented by investment advisers with a broad-brush scenario for the world economy. This may be impressive in its scope, but one employee trustee is quoted as saying that once he had heard two or three of these he realized that it was nothing more than one could pick up from a regular reading of the *Financial Times*.[16] However, given that pension funds are integrally bound up with the daily functioning of the economic and financial system, there are obviously major areas of familiarity with the mechanics of that system which cannot be summarily dismissed.

Employee trustees receive minimal training, a matter of a few days at most, perhaps in the form of a tour of the Stock Exchange and a few seminars. This raises two related points. First, participation in pension fund control points up in sharp relief the question of what sorts of skill representatives are expected to acquire: however generous the training provision, it is vacuous to suppose that they can become amalgams of the occupations just referred to, scaled-down stockbrokers-cum-bankers-cum-actuaries. Secondly, the control of content is important: although the independence of representative training may not be as contentious as it is for trade union representatives involved in orthodox collective bargaining, it cannot be assumed that employee trustees have merely to acquire already defined skills. We return to these issues in Chapter 9.

Organizational resources were identified earlier as obvious sources of power. In so far as employee trustees operate as part of a network of union representatives (although having specific functions and obligations), they may attempt to draw on their union for advice and expertise. The evidence is, however, that unions are as yet little prepared to provide a major service in this respect. With one or two exceptions they have not identified pensions trusteeship as an area where they seek to exercise a substantial amount of muscle. Traditionally unions have supported State pensions provision, and have only recently begun to take the initiative on pensions bargaining. To take on board at the same time the complex issues of fund control would tax their resources even at a time of union strength, and many trustees receive minimal support from this traditional source.

Ideology is a further factor. The practice of what might be called 'active capitalism'—i.e. individuals or institutions involving themselves actively in the affairs of the companies in which they have holdings, for whatever purpose—evokes little enthusiasm in the UK at large, certainly in comparison with the high level of financial activity exhibited within the City. Although trade unions are starting to press for involvement at company level in capital decisions this is within the framework of collective bargaining, and can be justified simply by the access it affords to information for bargaining purposes. Direct decision-making on capital allocation, especially where this is unconnected with their own industry, still evokes uncertainty and often hostility, even where overt opposition to capitalism, historically embodied in many union rule books, has been subdued. (This is reflected in the contrast with West Germany, where the unions have entered enthusiastically into financial management, directly owning the country's fifth biggest bank along with other very substantial assets.) There is, in short, a range of attitudes: some employee trustees are *plus royal que le roi*, energetically pursuing conventionally calculated rates of return for their investments; others exhibit ambivalence, attempting to reconcile instinctive distaste for financial management with their obligations to the members and their perceptions of a significant opportunity for control; others again reject the idea of participation of this kind, or attempt to convert it into orthodox bargaining.

Some of these factors are specific to the control of pension fund capital in the UK, with no broader application. Others, however, have a wider application. The unavailability of alternative techniques for the formulation of policy has confined representatives in many fields and at different levels to an essentially negative role, since they are unable to come forward themselves with positive proposals. The further the arena of decision-making is removed from the occupational experience of representatives, the more serious such a constraint is likely to be. Given that the management of capital is not a function in which many employees are involved on a regular basis, this does much to explain the limited impact of representation on the control of this key area.

Their power is further constrained by the broader structure of the financial system. Minns has traced out the tight network of bankers and brokers who handle the funds on behalf of the trustees.[17] A single merchant bank may act as adviser to a score or more of funds.

Moreover, the banking fraternity is close-knit, organizationally and culturally. In the same way, therefore, as interlocking directorates allow a smallish group to exercise substantial influence on the strategic decisions of a large number of companies,[18] so a close-knit network of financial managers folds itself round the decisions of trustees from a wide range of pension funds.

More broadly still, there is a growing debate about the theoretical scope for significant changes in the pattern of economic control. In part this is a natural evolution from the perception of a dominant finance sector within the British economy, but it has been given practical impetus by political initiatives for using pension fund capital to regenerate the economy, both nationally and regionally. In addition to the Labour party's proposal for a National Investment Bank drawing partly on pension funds, several Local Enterprise Boards have been set up, some of which intend to tap their own local-government superannuation fund and to encourage employee trustees on the boards of other funds to direct capital their way.

I do not wish to stray into theories of finance capital. The relevance of the debate for our purposes may be summarized as follows: on the one hand it is argued that financial institutions must follow the law of value, which entails maximum self-expansion by whatever means; their behaviour reflects rather than causes trends and crises in the productive sector, and therefore any attempts to exert democratic control over them put the cart before the horse. Against this it is argued—more plausibly in my view—that such a position ignores the difference between theoretical discussions of what the notion of money signifies in a capitalist society, and the effects in practice of the operations of existing financial institutions. It also ignores the tension between long-term and short-term calculations and underplays the scope for employee representatives (and others) to develop a significant influence on the investment policies of pension funds.[19]

Bearing in mind, then, the limited impact so far of employee representation on the control of capital, we can identify three potential strategies for the future. These may be pursued with different degrees of vigour and success. They may also be seen to overlap or to conflict with each other. This focus on an uncertain future is justified by the newness of participation in this area, by the significance of the capital sums involved, and by the evidence which suggests that the power of employee representatives grows directly with the accumulation of experience.

- *Active shareholder role.* Institutions have historically been loth to intervene in the companies in which they hold shares. There are signs that this is changing, and the Wilson Committee on the functioning of financial institutions recommended that they should take a more active interest. The US has a stronger tradition of active capitalism; employee influence there has been directed largely towards bringing pressure on to companies to conform to specified 'good employer' criteria, by, for example, recognizing trade unions and ensuring a healthy work environment. Intervention in the UK has been mainly restricted to substantive but one-off actions, such as the curbing of excessive managerial perks. Moreover it has been the managers of the funds rather than the trustees—still less the employee trustees—who have initiated the action. However, some funds have already acted to restructure management in organizations in which they are major shareholders, and it is not unlikely that employee trustees, especially those of the larger funds, will in the future be involved in decisions affecting the strategy of host companies.

- *Investment policy in individual funds.* Investment policy is to be distinguished from individual investment decisions. It concerns the allocation of the funds' assets, and revenues from them, between different sectors—gilts, equities, property, and so on—or between domestic and foreign investment. At present employee representatives play little part in the fashioning of investment policy. But given the funds' higher public exposure, there may now be awareness of a broader range of options available. Moreover, some trade unions are beginning to brief members who are trustees on policy stand-points, for example towards overseas investment or the purchase of public assets being 'denationalized'. Employee representatives may be urged to ensure that a portion of the fund be used not simply to earn revenue but also to regenerate industry. Pension scheme members, it is argued, would benefit from the higher level of economic activity, both as current or future pensioners and in their employment prospects.

- *Collective action.* The impact of a single fund, however big, on the economy at any level can only be marginal. It has therefore been suggested that employee representatives should institute co-ordinated action by several funds, for example in order to support Local Enterprise Boards' initiatives to achieve a kind of localized Keynesian reflation. Just as some would envisage in the production sphere corporatist bodies engaged in joint policy-making at industry and national level, so in the financial sphere there could be activity, with labour representation, above the level of the individual organization.[20]

Both the latter two strategies sharply illustrate, however, how misleading it would be to expect democratization to dispel tensions. There are major areas of investment which might command popular, democratic support and for which a clear case could also be made out on straightforward economic grounds. But the more particular the decision, the more difficult it is to refer to previously defined and socially agreed-upon criteria. What democratization can do, as we observed in the case of co-operatives, is broaden the options which are considered and the criteria for decision-making.

6 Determining the work environment

Health and safety is the classic counter to the charge that worker participation is not concerned with issues that matter to employees. It is easy to indulge in quasi-biblical rhetoric about the meaning of work; fulfilment is harder to achieve if you have lungs blackened by pneumoconiosis or a permanent splitting headache from the glare of a VDU—or if your job leaves you psychologically impaired. Employee influence over working conditions is neither a precondition nor a consequence of democratization but an integral component of it.

There is a massive literature on health and safety at work, documenting the causes of problems and the development of different strategies to cope with them.[1] In some cases, workers have pressed for direct State action to regulate working conditions, for instance by lobbying to achieve the passage of legislation governing the use of chemicals. They have also sought the means to regulate such questions themselves, through increased access to information, strengthened rights for safety representatives, or the establishment of joint health and safety committees. We shall focus on the second approach and especially the latter component, as exemplifying democracy at work.

This chapter refers mainly to 'health and safety'. But we begin with a review of the variety of ways of conceptualizing the issue which makes clear how its scope can be broadened to include the working environment more generally. The functioning of health and safety committees as joint decision-making bodies is then used to illustrate the problems of evaluating participation and to underline the implausibility of drawing a neat line between negotiation and consultation.

Conceptual trends in health and safety regulation

Health and safety go together like bacon and eggs—except that pigs are pigs, hens are hens, and though the product can vary greatly in quality and volume, its identity as a staple breakfast dish does not change much. Health and safety have each changed their identity over time, and their relation to each other has also changed. Although both the conjunction of the two and the order in which they come are now accepted as normal in the United Kingdom, this is not the case universally, nor has it been so in the past in this country. Earlier concern was focused explicitly on industrial accidents, and on safety simply as the absence or prevention of such events. Thus legislation put forward in 1953 was entitled the Employment (Inspection and Safety Organization) Bill. In 1970, health was tacked on in the Employed Persons (Safety and Health) Bill. It was not until the passage and implementation of the 1974 Health and Safety at Work Act that the current order was established. Such niceties of legislative nomenclature may seem trivial, and one can question how far health has really been given the priority suggested, but the changes do reflect conceptual developments which signal the way for more concrete progress.

The changes are not random, nor the result of philosophical reflection by the parliamentary clerks who draft legislation. They are the result of long direct experience and of struggles to broaden ideas about health and safety at work. To get an idea of the scope for change we can turn straight to Europe, where this process has been most significant at either end of the geographical pole: in Italy and Scandinavia.

In Italy changes were closely linked to the tumultuous political events of the late 1960s, though they had been gestating throughout the previous decade. Pressures developed to reject danger money as compensation for working in conditions likely to produce accidents, and moved beyond the notion of safety as merely protection against injuries. They culminated in the 1970 Workers Rights Law, which offered a quite explicit challenge to managerial control of the very idea of health. It criticized not only the adequacy of existing policies and the values and criteria on which they were based, but also the right of employers and their medical representatives to determine what should be considered as a healthy working environment. Doctors paid by management were no longer to have any power within the factories, and absenteeism would be certified by public health physicians; workers would have the right to call on their own experts, and to set up occupational health services within the plant under their own control.

Legal provisions were backed up by the establishment of so-called 'homogeneous groups', composed of workers who have a common identity through their jobs and aimed at fostering grass-roots control over health and safety. Their function is to assemble and utilize both factual information (on noise levels, toxins, etc.) and subjective experience (for example on stress effects), and to put the views of outside experts through a 'mutual valuation' process. This entails the assembled workers collectively expressing their views on how far the scientific views and results offered actually conform to their own experience. Underlying this was a push to establish the principle of 'non-delegation of control', i.e. that workers should evaluate their own working conditions and not rely on the conceptions and expertise of external professionals.[2]

A similar challenge to previous conceptions of health and safety emerged in Scandinavia, though less directly linked to political conflict. There was in the 1960s a growing recognition of the complexity of working life, and of the way different factors within the work environment interacted with each other. Simple notions of occupational safety were discarded, and the conception of health broadened to include ideas about the quality of job content and the democratic management of the work environment—all this without neglecting bread-and-butter safety questions. In 1977 Sweden and Norway both passed Work Environment Acts, which have considerable similarities, but Norway has assumed a particular pioneering role in this field. The very title of the Act indicates the breadth of its approach, insisting on the need to look at the workplace and the organization of work generally in devising solutions. Human mistakes—often used to attribute accidents to the 'careless worker'—are to be made less likely rather than penalized. Health and safety are taken to include psychological risks incurred at work, a conceptual breakthrough that changes the scope of the issue dramatically. Above all, there is an insistence on the need to generate grass-roots employee activity in relation to all work environment issues. In the planning of the work environment, health and safety issues are to be taken into account from the start, so that the occurrence rather than the effect of dangers is minimized. Safety representatives have the right to stop production if they consider that a danger is likely to occur in the future, not only if it is actually present. Work should be organized so as to utilize the employees' own abilities to control and improve working conditions, or, as the introduction of the Act's central section 12 puts it, 'so that the employees are not exposed to undesirable physical or mental strain and so that their possibilities of displaying caution and observing safety measures are not impaired'. On precisely this principle there was a massive educational campaign, using the famous Scandinavian study circle technique, to publicize the provisions of the Act and to encourage an active worker response.[3] Approaching 10 per cent of the entire labour force (over 150,000 out of 1.9 million) have been involved in structured discussions of this kind.

We can relate these points to the various conceptions of participation outlined at the beginning of the book. Clearly the thrust of both the Italian and the Scandinavian initiatives is to shift the frontiers of control by promoting direct participation at plant level, as well as indirect participation at industry and national level. They involve workers in the regulation of a part of their working lives which is of immediate and substantive interest, but the implications of this also impinge significantly on longer-term decisions. (The banning of asbestos in industrial production, for example, has major implications for design and investment decisions governing future production processes.) In principle at least, the expansion of the scope of health and safety brings in worker representation at an earlier stage in the decision-making process. And since the State has for some time assumed a responsibility for the health of its citizens, its role has been relatively pronounced in this area and provides a significant example of how legal requirements can be a source of power.

This century has seen in the UK a string of Acts or proposed Acts relating to health and safety, many of which contained some reference to worker representation. At one level this was confined to the initiation of inspections: for instance the 1911 Coal Mines Act allowed workers to appoint any two persons to inspect the mine—at their own expense. The 1954 Mines and Quarries Act gave unions the right to appoint a panel for inspection purposes, though a Department of Trade survey showed how dependent legislation is on other factors for its effectiveness: there were 14 inspections per mine in 1969 compared with 0.08 per quarry. Size of work-force is part of the explanation, but the cohesion and strength of the miners' union was undoubtedly needed to give proper effect to the law.[4] The 1961 Factories Act—later, but not dealing specifically with such undeniably dangerous occupations and therefore weaker—gave representatives no rights to inspect records, liaise with HM Inspectorate, or obtain particular information concerning hazards. (One right it did give them was the rather macabre one of attending inquests.)

Consultation on a voluntary basis has also been long canvassed as a means of involvement. In 1918 the Health of Munition Workers' Committee suggested that worker committees should be set up to study the causes of accidents and to suggest ways of preventing them, but the voluntary nature of the approach meant that there were few practical developments. The parallel with Whitley councils is fairly obvious: immediate post-war concern, voluntarist proposals, little action. This pattern was repeated after the Second World War in line with other participation initiatives, as we have seen in Chapter 3.[5] All the post-war nationalization Acts contained obligations to set up joint accident prevention machinery, but all avoided compulsion.[6] The narrow remit of the proposed initiatives is also noteworthy.

The sluggishness of response to pleas for voluntary action has been long documented. As far back as 1927 employer resistance to the proposal for compulsory committees in those industries with high accident rates was strong enough to secure its withdrawal on the understanding that the number of voluntary committees would increase rapidly; thirty years later, they were still awaited in many factories, being almost non-existent in smaller ones with under 100 employees.[7] A 1978 survey investigated the extent and nature of the joint committees which existed before the 1974 Act established their formation on a statutory basis. It found that under half (44 per cent) of the 970 establishments surveyed had had such committees. Not surprisingly, these were concentrated in the industries with high accident rates, so their existence can be explained as an 'adaptive response'; the survey also found, however, that a strong trade union presence was a significant explanatory factor.[8]

Legislation, then, was successfully resisted or emasculated for a long time. Sidney Webb's characterization of an earlier era applies equally well to recent history:

This century of experiment in factory legislation allows a typical example of English [*sic*] practical empiricism. We began with no practical theory of social justice or the rights of man. We seem always to have been incapable even of taking a general view of the subject we were legislating upon.[9]

Procrastination has carried right through to modern times. Both in 1970 and 1974 bills dealing with health and safety were before Parliament but fell because a general election was called. Finally in 1974 the Health and Safety at Work Act reached the statute-book. Although essentially an enabling measure, the Act broke new ground in setting a statutory basis for employee involvement: it immediately provided for employee safety representatives to be appointed (amended by the 1975 Employment Protection Act so that the appointment should be through recognized trade unions only), and paved the way for joint committees, obliging the employer to establish one within three months if so requested by at least two safety representatives.

We consider the effect of this statutorily based move to participation in the next section, but it is worth stressing that there is no tidy, if prolonged, prógression through to a resting-place in the statute-book. The drafting, passage, and even the successful initial implementation of legislation are not enough to guarantee an irreversible advance in health and safety standards, nor worker participation in their administration. Recent history in the US provides an excellent example. The 1970 Occupational Safety and Health Act made worker participation mandatory in the setting and enforcement of standards and in decisions on appeals. As a national initiative it represented a radical departure from previous American practice, which had left the issue up to individual States. After the passage of the Act came a period of development, involving the setting of standards, the initiation of union representatives into the mystique of public testifying, and the general accumulation of expertise. Stage two, from 1977 to 1980, saw the implementation of the Act through the establishment of resource centres to train professionals appropriately and acquaint representatives with research; the development of hazard evaluation and the implementation of standards already set; and improved communication between Safety and Health Administration officials, academics, and labour representatives. Until recently, therefore, the Act could be perceived as a substantial, if not unqualified, advance. The advent of a conservative Republican administration, however, proved that legislation can be nullified without being actually removed from the statute-books: there has been since 1980 procrastination in the further setting of standards, and a reduction in the resources devoted to the resource centres and the spreading of expertise and awareness. Specifically on the issue of participation, moreover, workers have been discouraged from playing a part in inspections.

In short, health and safety provides an example of a struggle over law as a power resource in the operation of participation. Yet it is not unambiguous as a resource. Arguably the passage of legislation in some ways weakens labour, who are induced to abandon organizational for juridical strengths. Such a line of reasoning lies behind many unions' preference for relying on safety representatives rather than safety committees (though the former also received statutory backing from the 1974 Act). Safety representatives are free to act more according to the canons of traditional trade unionism, with more direct links to such industrial muscle as is available. Reliance on joint committees, by contrast, shifts the mode of decision-making somewhat away from negotiation. The relatively high expectation that a law shall be implemented induces an unwarranted sense of security, and diminishes employer responsibility. Certainly the legal resource is effective only if mobilized in conjunction with others, and a true analysis of decision-making on health and safety must encompass the interaction between legal, organizational, economic, and even philosophic trends.

The effect of participation: joint health and safety committees

Apart from the development of a cadre of safety representatives, the most significant form of participation has been the growth of health and safety committees. Most establishments now have such a committee, and the incidence in larger workplaces is very high (roughly three out of four). Although many committees already existed before the 1974 Act gave representatives the right to require their establishment, the practical effect of the right is testified to by the substantial proportion of committees which were introduced only after its passage.

The widespread incidence of joint committees tells us little about the nature and effectiveness of participation. In this section we deal with the issues surrounding the definition of 'successful' participation, and then with some more specific aspects of its functioning.

Accounts of participation tend in general to be enthusiastic about its impact. Blumberg's conclusion is often quoted (though commentary since has been more probing and often more sceptical): 'There is scarcely a study in the entire literature which fails to demonstrate that satisfaction in work is enhanced or that other generally acknowledged beneficial consequences accrue from a genuine increase in workers' decision-making power.'[10] To some extent, this rosiness reflects an inevitable bias towards reporting the successful and allowing the failures to slide quietly under the surface. Some of the accounts exhibit great methodological *naïveté*, ignoring the so-called Hawthorne effect[11] and using very simplistic measuring techniques. Many are carried out very close to the implementation of the exercise and therefore cannot include the extent to which the putative effects persist over time. The most common type of claim is that absenteeism and labour turnover drop, productivity and job satisfaction jump, and all parties are seen to have benefited. This may indeed be the case, but it is rare that the objectives and outcomes of participation can be so clearly defined or so easily framed in a unitary perspective.

Health and safety seems to provide a counter-example to the view that management and labour engage in joint decision-making with fundamentally different goals. This point was made unreservedly by the Robens Committees, which was set up in the early 1970s to report on safety and health at work:

There is a greater mutual identity of interest between 'the two sides' in relation to safety and health problems than in most other matters. There is no legitimate scope for bargaining on safety and health issues but much scope for constructive discussion, joint inspection and participation in working out solutions.[12]

Clearly it is true in the broadest sense that some objectives will be shared, even if they are given different weightings and different motives are involved. Moreover, the record is open to quantification. The reduction of deaths and mutilations can be counted and would be subscribed to by all—even by the most callous employer, since they are disruptive of production and disturb the work-force. Surely, then, an effective health and safety committee can be judged by its impact on the accident rate and safety record of the plant it covers.

Yet evaluation is difficult. Although the record appears to be positive, it is as hard in the case of health and safety as in other areas to disentangle the effect of participation from all the other intervening variables. Leaving aside methodological problems, however, the apparently straightforward nature of the issue is deceptive. The problems can be classified as of two kinds.

The first relates to the way the goals are defined. We have already described the struggles which have taken place over the scope of regulations and legislation, and pointed to the significance of the clumsy zeugma: to restrict attention to 'safety' by looking only at the accident record is to rule out the wider considerations which 'health' suggests. Furthermore, health can be interpreted negatively or—as the World Health Organization emphatically recommends—as a positive state of 'physical, psychological and spiritual well-being'. In the latter case the implications for action and reform are liable to be more profound—and more costly to the company in immediate economic terms. The inclusion of psychological as well as physical factors adds a further dimension with immense implications. So the definition of what is to be measured is a major potential source of conflict.

Now this might be widely recognized, but the counter-argument put forward is that it is simply a matter of progressing from the immediate consensus surrounding physical safety to the eventual establishment of a truly healthy work environment. As resources become available, they can be used to make gradual but steady progress. But this not only implicitly recognizes that there is a distributive issue involved, since the resources devoted at any time to health cannot be used elsewhere; it also ignores the fact that a trade-off is entailed between different groups of employees (present and future), who stand to benefit or lose according to the rate of change and improvement. As in the case of pensions, different time-horizons yield different, and often competing, definitions of interests.

There is, then, inherent tension in the setting of objectives. Under any system there will be pressures on producers—whether from the consumer, the planner, or from themselves—to produce cheaply and quickly, at the possible expense of safety and health. The question is therefore one of *relative* priorities; what is an 'acceptable' risk, given that risk can be envisaged in any occupation? That said, the constraints and pressures of the major capitalist imperative, private profit, are dangerous in a wholly literal sense, exacerbating the tension between production and health.

Secondly, there is the question of the way in which participation is to operate in order for the goals to be achieved. One option is for the participative body to take direct action itself as far as possible, initiating changes, banning dangerous practices, and penalizing transgressors. This obviously makes it easier to attribute impact to participation, but the approach has potential drawbacks. In the first place, action may then be left to the particular body. Senior managers have criticized the setting up of health and safety committees on the grounds that it gives line management the impression that the issue is no longer their responsibility, and so diminishes overall concern and effort. The higher the committee's profile, the more it will be assumed—at all levels—to be coping with the problems itself. Whilst members of the committee may relish this, and report very positively on their experience of participation, the concentration of responsibility in their hands may diminish the overall effort to an extent that outweighs its own contribution. Health and safety committees do not have the kind of broad-ranging powers necessary to deal with the work environment as a whole, as they are generally excluded from taking decisions with major financial implications. It is therefore important for those involved in making decisions elsewhere in the organization to be made aware of health and safety issues.

One further possible consequence should be noted. Participation may result in labour assuming greater responsibility for disciplining itself—'self-management' in the literal sense—without the causes of the problems being tackled. The committee becomes at least in part a means of relieving management of its disciplinary function. This is particularly likely when accidents are caused by 'careless workers', the solution therefore being to modify the behaviour of the workers rather than to ask why they find themselves in circumstances in which accidents are liable to occur.

The alternative is for participation to act as a leavener, a means of raising consciousness throughout the workplace. This is in itself a form of behaviour modification, but it can also serve to promote awareness and elicit contributions from the work-force on how the environment might be improved. A major new resource is thereby mobilized—though once again the form it takes will depend heavily on the way health and safety is defined and causation is analysed. This alternative is not necessarily in opposition to the first. For example, stress could be laid on the need for representatives involved in committees to acquire particular skills of communication and mobilization, so that they keep their members informed of the committee's activities and encourage them to take a positive interest themselves in the work environment. But there is a tension, particularly well documented in the case of health and safety but extending to other forms of participation, between the development of a properly informed, resourced, and effectively involved set of representatives on the one hand, and the tendency on the other of such a development to lower the contributions made by rank-and-file individuals not involved in the participative body. The working environment of these latter may improve to some extent, but given the demonstrated link between impact and depth of activity, the overall effect is likely to be less than it might have been.

The acquisition by representatives of special skills and knowledge is dealt with in Chapter 9.[13] But this kind of 'professionalization' has its counterpart on the managerial side, and health and safety illustrates it neatly. To set this in context we need briefly to set out the determinants of effective committees, as far as they have been identified in current research. As with the constraints on the effectiveness of pensions participation summarized in the last chapter, some of these are specific to the issue of health and safety whilst others are of wider application.

Interpreting effectiveness narrowly, in terms of ability to get things done and to affect workplace relationships, and looking only at the functioning of the committee itself rather than external factors such as varying industry accident rates or plant size, we can point to the following factors. The committee should be of an appropriate size, not unwieldy, but on the other hand large enough to accommodate diverse representation, especially where there are several unions. Like the committee itself, the agenda must be neither unwieldy nor too constricted. Similarly there should be democratic access in the sense of freedom to attach items to the agenda. The scheduling of meetings is relevant. Obviously committees that meet every six months can have little direct impact. Nevertheless it is regularity rather than frequency which appears to count. The presence of a senior manager indicates commitment. It gives authority to the committee and encourages employees as well as other managers to take it seriously. Technical expertise is a further source of power. Professional assistance can provide valuable support and impetus to the committee. Both professional and lay participants are likely to require initial and recurrent training.[14]

It is the last two items on this list that are most relevant here. Extensive training is one of the defining characteristics of the professional status towards which many occupations strive (see Chapter 7). Safety officers show every sign of following the well-beaten path of professionalization, setting up their own institute, asserting their autonomous status, and developing their own body of knowledge. This may very well assist their own effectiveness in improving the work environment, but it raises two particular issues.

First is the prospect of tension between the desire of professionals for autonomy on the one hand, and their place in a particular authority structure on the other. Safety officers have a vested interest in giving health and safety status within the organization, and in protecting it, for example against the pressures of production managers. But they do not normally occupy senior management positions, and are answerable as subordinates to their hierarchical superiors. The fact that they contribute substantially to the effectiveness of a joint body does not mean that their primary commitment is to it. Secondly, they are also answerable to the participative body concerned with their area of expertise. They have an incentive to increase its effectiveness. Yet professionalization increases the desire to be judged by one's peers alone, the corollary being a diminished readiness to accept the judgements of untrained (or 'amateur') people. The growth of a codified body of competence to which there is restricted access may generate tension between the democratic functioning of the committee and its technically defined effectiveness. So safety officers, as they themselves become more specialized and qualified, reduce their expectations of what the committee (or the work-force as a whole) can contribute. *Mutatis mutandis* these points may apply to many other participative bodies; and the inherent pressures towards further division of bureaucratic as well as occupational labour (decision-making bodies as well as jobs) makes likely the emergence in other areas of roles equivalent to that of the safety officer in health and safety.[15]

Consultation and participation: fuzzy oscillation

We have looked briefly at how health and safety illustrates the problems of defining the *goals* of participation, and of *how* these goals are to be achieved. We turn, finally, to the way health and safety exemplifies the protean character of participation.

It is not only academics who like to put things into boxes. The attempt by the Robens Committee to define health and safety squarely as an area of joint problem-solving by excluding negotiation has already been cited. The obverse would be to argue that it is a negotiable item in exactly the same way as pay is. A health and safety committee might be seen as 'merely' consultative, for example, because it has no power over financial resources. Yet the evidence is that the topic stubbornly refuses to recognize institutional boundaries. The uncertainty is threefold.

First, different parties may seek to impose different interpretations of what they are doing. Typically, management will wish to define the process as consultative, whilst unions will be keen at least that negotation should be possible. So there may be a *simultaneous* variation of conception.

Secondly, the process may vary *over time*. Sometimes it is more appropriately characterized as negotiation, and sometimes as consultation. Representatives have described themselves as 'moving up a gear', shifting out of a consultative into a negotiating stance as required, as part of the normal process. All parties may agree this to be the case, though the first uncertainty may still persist as management and unions draw the line at different points.

Thirdly, differences of view over the nature of the process at a given moment may be linked to broader questions of *future* behaviour. As Flanders has observed, 'When union representatives claim the right to be consulted, they are more often than not demanding an opportunity to negotiate *should the need for it arise*' (my stress). In other words, analysis of a particular event or activity depends on its relation to some unspecified event or activity in the future, which may in practice never be realized.

I have already described the move to broaden the health and safety issue, so that accidents and ill health are set in the overall context of the work environment, and attention is switched away from isolated incidents and on to labour as a continuing process. But breadth is not the only dimension. Historically, health and safety efforts have been directed almost exclusively towards short-term problems which make themselves felt in acute form. Now there is, at least in principle, more widespread recognition that the major dangers are to be found in *long-term* exposure to risks and an unhealthy environment.

This crucially affects approaches to health and safety in two ways. First, it alters the balance between prevention and cure, pushing those responsible into looking to the future instead of reacting to events which have already taken place, or which are so imminent that they are virtually in the present. Secondly, it demands that attention be paid to the *cumulative* effects of work. A job or a feature of the work environment which is perfectly harmless over a short period, say one year, can have a highly injurious effect if it is maintained for long stretches. By extending the time-frame over which the judgement is made, the very conception of 'labour' is changed. No longer is the worker an anonymous ahistorical entity who simply happens to be present and impinged upon contingently by a given hazard; instead, he or she is an identifiable person with a past and a present as well as, one hopes, a future.

7 Political and industrial democracy

There is, on the face of it, a direct opposition between the obligations of elected representatives to the voters who elect them and the scope for public employees to control their own work. Should school dinner ladies decide on what sort of school meals service is offered, or Permanent Secretaries on the size of their departments, given that they have already had the chance to participate in the democratic process which installed their political masters? Should the claims of public employees to a say over their working environment be wholly subordinated to the political mandate of an elected administration? Are the two types of democracy, political and industrial, incompatible? This chapter will argue that the antithesis is not so much false as greatly oversimplified, and will explore how participation is shaped by the distinctive forms of power distribution within the public service.

The discussion will refer principally to public services, and especially to governmental services at national and local level. Other parts of the public sector, such as nationalized industries, raise some of the same issues. But since they operate in the traded sector of the economy, they resemble in many respects their private counterparts, for example in drawing up conventional profit and loss sheets. In public administration, however strenuous the attempts to import performance criteria and management techniques from the private sector, decision-making cannot be determined by the constraints which characteristically shape organizational goals in the private or public traded sectors. Our discussion will centre round employment in national and local government, with intermittent reference to other public services such as the National Health Service.[1]

The key feature, immediately and intuitively apparent, is that the organization is already under formal democratic control. Employees are subject not to owners of capital or their appointed representatives, but to elected members of local or national political bodies. Hence the claim of democratic principle—that people's enfranchised status should not be stripped from them as they walk into office, shop, or factory—does not apply. They can all (with the exception of employees under 18) vote for those who they wish to see in power and take part in the political processes in which elections are embedded: the formulation of party policies, the selection of representatives, and so on. For public employees to aspire to full participation at work is to ask for a double vote. Moreover, so the argument goes, if public employees gain a significant measure of workplace control they will be able to plunder the common exchequer, as if they had access to a publicly supplied slot-machine which returned the coin each time it was inserted. The idea that public servants, whose work is subject neither to market constraints nor other putatively objective measurement techniques, should determine their own working conditions is seen as a recipe for unregulated syndicalism.

The distinction has validity. Whatever one's cynicism about the degree of democracy embodied within a particular political system, the State as employer is accountable to its citizenry, amongst whom are its employees, in a way that private employers are not. There are, of course, major limitations on its accountability: the cumbersome and secretive nature of the political process, the unequal influence exercised by different classes, and the time-lag between decisions and the electoral judgement on them, to name but three. Nevertheless, employees cannot claim to be totally excluded as they are (at least as individuals) in the private sector. We need to look at why the issue has emerged, reflect briefly on the nature of the State, and then turn to the actors in the decision-making process.

Servants or employees?

Historically, there has been a general reluctance to contemplate employee participation in governmental services. Collective bargaining was already well established in the Civil Service early in this century, and there has—until very recently—been no serious challenge to the right to negotiate, even if the practice has often been complex.[2] In public corporations there is also a long tradition of formal participative initiatives, and many of the parliamentary Acts on nationalization contain specific clauses enjoining management to establish forms of industrial democracy (for example the Transport Act of 1947, the Post Office Act in 1969, and the Shipbuilding and Aircraft Act in 1977). In public administration, however, there has naturally been no similar opportunity to convert decision-making structures along with ownership.

It is true that Whitley Councils began life mainly in the public sector. But this was because private employers refused to be told to introduce participation by a government which was itself inactive on this front. It was only to prevent the scheme from collapsing altogether that the government made itself the reluctant exemplar of good practice. Moreover, Whitley first considered participation in the Civil Service only in relation to those government establishments where conditions were closely analogous to industrial concerns outside.[3] Subsequent debates on participation have tended to ignore public administration altogether, to suggest that it raises no qualitatively different issues, or to acknowledge its peculiarity and pass over it very summarily.[4] However awkward, the issue is salient for a number of reasons.

First is the straightforward growth in the number of people employed in government. In the UK, employees in this sector now form over one-fifth of the total working population. Local-government employment alone topped 3 million in 1980, amounting to over 12 per cent of the total labour force, and the pattern is repeated in other countries. Government employees are no longer a minority work-force who can be more or less reasonably ignored because of their peculiar circumstances.[5]

Secondly, these circumstances are no longer as peculiar as they were. The shift from 'public servant' to 'public employee' is more than terminological. The relative advantage enjoyed by government workers over their private counterparts has largely disappeared. The hallmark of a nineteenth-century civil servant was his entitlement to a pension. State pensions are now universal and occupational ones widespread; and even if index-linked civil service pensions are still a substantial material benefit, they no longer denote a qualitatively different employment status. Other benefits, such as annual paid holidays, have also rippled outwards so that only those with marginal employment status are excluded. Although the evidence on pay is not clear-cut, public employees tend to suffer in times of high inflation because of the time-lags involved in reaching agreements. Even the security of employment which once characterized public service has been regularly breached: after the events of recent years manual local-government employees would look with jaundiced eyes at the argument that they should abandon claims to participative rights because as public servants their jobs are secure. Finally, the quality of working life is no longer differentiated from that of the private sector by its relative serenity and structure. The job of a benefits clerk in a social security office is certainly not insulated from outside realities; nor does it offer substantial career opportunities.[6]

Closely related to this the growth of public-service trade unions and of militancy within them. Set against the decline of the traditional unions, the phenomenon has grown even more in relative than in absolute importance within the labour movement. Historically, white-collar public servants have unionized earlier than their private-sector counterparts, and the changed balance of union membership towards white-collar workers strongly reflects the expansion of governmental services. Simple numbers tell a poor story, however. Becoming a union member does not necessarily signify a major ideological conversion, especially when it is part of a closed-shop agreement. But though there is some evidence that 'unionateness' (whole-hearted commitment to trade unionism) is less prevalent amongst government workers,[7] militancy has spread rapidly if unevenly. Public-sector industrial relations, as a whole, have deteriorated significantly over the last decade, partly as a consequence of the longer-run factors outlined above and partly because of the abrupt imposition and perceived inequity of a cash limits system. Industrial action is now taken by groups of public-service workers of whom such behaviour would have been inconceivable not long ago.

The growth of the sector, the convergence between its conditions of employment and those of other sectors, and the concomitant shift in employee behaviour and attitudes make it impossible to exclude public-service employment from discussion of democratic rights at work. The notion of the State as standing in some quasi-feudal relation to its employees, giving them the guarantee of secure and relatively privileged conditions of work in return for deferential service, no longer obtains.

The management of public service

The role of the State has attracted much attention in political theory, but far less in industrial relations.[8] The notion of the State as even-handedly holding the ring between interest groups and discharging an essentially administrative role, its employees thus being 'functionaries' in the literal sense, has been sharply confronted by a complex set of criticisms, mainly neo-Marxist in origin. Some view the State as simply representing capitalist interests at the expense of the working class. For others, the State, in its various cultural, economic, and regulative guises, has no simple and unambiguous function. It has to ensure production, and the successful reproduction of conditions for that production, by regulating the economy and providing the appropriate social and welfare services. Such operations ultimately assist the accumulation of capital, and the role of public servants must be interpreted accordingly.

However, as Dearlove observes:

Their formulation, which suggests that state intervention is functional for capital as a whole and in the long run, not only raises the question of what exactly is the long run but also begs the question of the sort of analysis that is appropriate to the shorter run.[9]

This type of perception leads to a more nuanced view of the State as itself reflecting the multiple and temporally differentiated tensions and conflicts of society generally. The tensions within the State, and between its own 'fractions' and 'fractions' of capital, can then be traced out, and the unevenness of the impact of State activity on social groups and structures explored.[10]

The role of the State has become the subject of mounting and immediate political debate. The so-called New Right has chosen this as the terrain on which to flex their new-found muscle, challenging the post-war consensus on the politically tolerable minimum level of public services. For them, accountability is to be found through market mechanisms alone, even though their description of how such mechanisms would work is crude in the extreme. From sections of the Left comes a critique of existing State practice and a call for new forms of accountability to its citizens and clients. These are often only loosely sketched out, appearing as a combination of greater decentralization and the involvement of a wider range of citizen groups. Caught in the middle are the more pragmatic reformists, who argue for forms of accountability which do not depend wholly either on the market or on political activism. The intensity of political feeling makes it both particularly difficult to take a measured view of the implications for the role of public employees, and particularly important to do so.

Views of the State's relation to 'its' people have generally considered the latter as citizens, taxpayers, or consumers of public services. 'Participation' in the context of State activity normally refers to citizen, not employee, participation. Yet just as the State is not a neutral administrative entity, so its role as employer is neither simple nor passive. We should not expect to find it operating as a pure model employer (though governments have come to accept some obligation to act as 'good employers') nor as an archetypal exploiter of labour. Its diverse components exhibit a variety of employment practices, depending on a mixture of factors: the nature of their activity (compare the army with a social security office), the political complexion of elected members, the degree of direct contact with the clients or consumers, and so forth. Not only is there variety; there will in all probability be inconsistency and contradictions. We can look only summarily at three elements, all ambiguous, which shape the nature of the employment relationship and the scope for participation.

First, the *political colour* of the elected administration and the attitudes and qualities of individual politicians will impinge on the character of employment relations within the State. It might be supposed that socialists lean more towards encouraging industrial democracy as a matter of political principle. Moreover, politicians with proclaimed links to the working classes have an ideological reason for seeking to support them in opposition to senior management, even though all are employees of the State. Conservatives, on the other hand, may wish to demonstrate an anti-State ideology by equating efficiency with the reduction of the rights as well as the numbers of public employees, and establishing as far as possible the market as the institution which determines the nature of the service.

This is, however, too simplistic. Some socialists will be dedicated to notions of corporate efficiency, or insist on a high degree of external accountability to safeguard the image of public services and public expenditure. The interests of public employees will then be subordinated to these goals. On the other hand, conservatives or liberals may subscribe to a unitary viewpoint which sees no conflict between efficiency and employee satisfaction. Especially at local-government level they may see the administration's employing role as a paternalist one, with strong emphasis on consultation. Furthermore, politicians generally will vary in the degree to which they wish or feel able to intervene actively in management policy. Many will simply give greater priority to extracting benefit for their own constituents or clientele than to overall organizational style.

If the nature of the public-sector employment relationship has changed and the State cannot be seen as a set of neutral administrative organizations, what are the implications for *managerial behaviour and attitudes*, especially in relation to participation? There is evidence of a convergence between management styles within public administration and those of the private sector, with management conceived of as a technical skill based on certain scientific principles derived directly from industrial organization. The extent to which government has followed business is uncertain, but some techniques have been unmistakably imported. Certainly at the ideological level this has been the case in America, where changes in the structure of federal, State, and local government have been justified by reference to the concept of 'scientific management'.[11] A review of local-government management in Britain concludes that it has been and still is derived from business organization and practice, notably with the adoption of corporate planning and PPBS (programme, planning, and budgeting system) both pioneered in the business world.[12] The introduction in 1980 of MINIS (Management Information System for Ministers) is an example of the phenomenon at central level and it has been given substantial impetus by the drive of privatization at all levels of government service (from local dustmen to government meteorological services), and by the explicit promotion of internal reviews using private-sector techniques. The way has been made easier for this approach by the relative inability of the public sector to develop its own distinctive management techniques, and by the political failure of Labour administrations to demonstrate how they reconcile the goals of efficiency, public service, and the setting of distinctively non-capitalist employment conditions.

Nevertheless, there are substantial differences in management styles between the public and private sectors, due to a mixture of politics and the nature of the activities concerned. At least until the recent deterioration of public-sector industrial relations, management was generally disposed to promote consultation within a markedly unitary perspective. The Whitley tradition was reinforced by several other factors: the absence of market pressures, the highly developed internal career structure, the general 'good employer' obligation, and the above-average level of labour intensity which makes the personnel function more important. Moreover the nature of decision-making itself has been contrasted with the private sector as relatively long-term, cautious, centralized, and goal-diffuse.[13] There is therefore a combination of general and particular features which makes it implausible to align public-sector management fully with private practice.

Specific evidence on participation points in a similar direction, though not unanimously. Local-authority management is reported to be relatively favourable to employee participation, and not only at lower levels.[14] Some local authorities have taken initiatives to circumvent the law which debars employees from formal membership of their committees by co-opting representatives or setting up parallel bodies. Agreements on new technology—identified earlier as one of the ways in which collective bargaining is being extended—are initially to be found more in local government than other sectors.[15] On the other hand, the most recent broad survey of workplace industrial relations suggests that consultative arrangements are more highly developed in nationalized industries then in the private sector, but less so in public administration.[16] Moreover, when it comes to strategic decisions, there is little evidence that managements are any more enthusiastic about worker representation than they are in the private sector—as we see in the case of the Post Office in Chapter 8.

There is a further problem which can here be only recognized rather than explored. The operations of the public sector are closely intertwined with those of the private sector. The former reacts to the latter's demands (though not necessarily obediently), strives to shape and guide some of its development, and exchanges personnel with it (though less so in the UK than in most countries). Decision-making in public administration is continuously impinged upon at almost every level by trends and events in the private sector. The notion of an insulated bureaucracy conducting its own operations ignores this interrelation and the influence it has on public-service ideologies and behaviour.

Public employees as a general category have a threefold relationship to the State: as employees, as citizens, and as consumers or clients of services. Underlying the basic argument against greater participation is the assumption that these three roles are in conflict with each other. To some extent this is true, but the nature of each of the roles needs to be examined more closely. As clients they may be currently in receipt of particular services (for example, as parents of children at school), prospective or past users (as parents of children not yet at or beyond school age), or non-users (without children). Moreover they will be paying different levels of local and national taxes. As citizens they may be politically opposed to State provision yet believe in high levels of public expenditure on areas such as law and order or defence. Conversely, they may have an ideological belief in the merits of public over private services, linked with a desire to see these operate as efficiently as possible both for intrinsic reasons and to sustain the general case for public provision. All these factors influence their attitudes to public services, and hence, as employees, to their work; and underline the impossibility of dividing off people's work experience from their social and domestic environments.[17]

The employee role itself contains ambiguities. Rather than exploit participation to feather-bed themselves at the expense of the taxpayer and consumer, employees might themselves be interested in providing as good a service as possible. There is no necessary zero-sum game whereby increased democratization means lower quality of service. To the extent that the State is perceived as extracting maximum effort from its work-force for the minimum reward, i.e. as the archetypal capitalist, this will be the case. Yet employees may be willing and able to improve their own working conditions and at the same time give effective public service.

Clearly, however, the categories of 'management' and 'employee' cannot be neatly separated; nor can the categories of political and administrative decisions.[18] The division of labour and the division of authority are interrelated in complex ways, and we turn in conclusion to two overlapping groups in the public-service sector who demonstrate this with particular salience. The role of *senior* civil servants and local-government officials illustrates one form of what can be called 'occupational participation'—direct participation in policy formulation by virtue of one's formal position within the occupational hierarchy. The role of *professionally qualified* workers illustrates a more implicit form: the assertion of their occupational expertise by members of a particular occupational group, as a means of determining the character of service provision according to their own criteria.

Formal occupational participation: senior officials

In most organizations, people in higher occupational categories are involved qua employees in decisions on issues where the participation of other categories of employee would denote a significant measure of democracy. The division of labour endows certain employee groups with substantial routine power of this kind, and this is particularly significant in the public services.

Government characteristically exhibits a more formalized and rigid division of labour than most bureaucracies. The Northcote Trevelyan Report of 1853, hallowed in Civil Service circles, proposed the establishment of a proper distinction between 'intellectual' and 'mechanical' labour. It was followed by the Playfair Report in 1874, which advocated a threefold distinction between clerical, executive, and administrative grades. The administrative grade was to be concerned with the formulation of policy and the control of public-service departments. From very early days, therefore, a category of governmental employee had influence on strategic decision-making built into its occupational definition.

The hierarchical division of labour makes it impossible to define a cut-off point beyond which employees shall have no influence on governmental decisions. Involvement in the highest reaches of policy formulation is simply part of the job for senior officials. They are, to be sure, not participating in any formal representative capacity, but they have the opportunity to influence decisions which affect both their own work and that of many others in their department.

Involvement of this broad type is unavoidable in a complex society with a substantial bureaucracy. But it is a form of direct participation which means that a theoretical, dichotomous question—are government employees entitled or not to participate in policy decisions?—must be transformed into a broader enquiry which covers the justification for giving authority to some categories of employee and not to others.

In the private sector the identity of the decision-making authority is in principle clear, in spite of the complex relationships between owners and managers. Ownership rights are a basic source of authority, and managements organize production in given ways as representatives of capital. Ownership rights do not exist in the same way in the public sector (despite the tendency of most Chancellors of the Exchequer to talk as if they personally disburse tax cuts from out of their own pockets).

Formally, elected politicians—MPs and councillors—propose, and civil servants and local government officials dispose. But the relationship between elected members and senior officials is not to be deduced from a reading of the constitution. Some commentators, indeed, directly reverse the conventional roles and depict the officials as policy-makers, with politicians carrying out routine administration through their committee work.[19] This is too neat an inversion, but its plausibility underlines the indeterminacy of practical authority. Certainly the official has a number of potent sources to draw on: professional expertise, continuity of experience, tradition, manpower, and so forth (manpower in the sense of being able to mobilize the department's resources in order to generate information and arguments in support of a case). Against this the politician has part of a political manifesto to brandish, a degree of personal authority, and perhaps also some direct expertise.

Their relationship with elected members places senior officials in an ambiguous position. They sit at the apex of departments which commonly employ huge numbers of people, yet are themselves formally servants of the government. In one sense, therefore, they are both employer and employee, manager and managed. Even as managers, however, they may be more concerned with managing the politicians to whom they are formally responsible than the members of their own department.[20]

There are naturally parallels with the private sector, where senior management are also formally employees and also determine strategy in varying degrees of independence from stockholders or external directors. But there is a peculiar degree of paradox inherent in the position of senior government officials, deriving from the contrast between their permanence and the transitoriness of elected members. On the one hand this appears to endow them with greater authority, as they endure whilst their political masters are ejected. On the other hand, this divergence itself reduces the degree to which they can ground their authority firmly on the political mandate of the elected administration. This is the more significant since, as we have seen, their authority has no basis in ownership rights.

The involvement of senior officials in policy formulation has two implications for our view of the relation between political and industrial democracy. In so far as it exists, it denotes a significant form of participation—which we have called 'occupational'—since senior officials are themselves public employees. It is, of course, not unique to them but it has a particular salience in the public-service context since it invalidates the dichotomous approach of a simple and direct opposition between political and industrial democracy. Secondly, it weakens the argument against more general public-service participation that employees have already had their say through the ballot-box. Departmental heads are not accountable to their subordinates even to the formal extent that their political masters are, and the electoral link between public servant and public master is abolished.

Professional determinism

Public services employ a high proportion of professionally qualified people. This refers in the broad sense to administrative classes with general degree-level qualifications, but also more specifically to occupations such as teaching or social work, whose members are mainly employed in local government, and to parts of the health service. Professionals, however defined, are members of occupational groups which enjoy a relatively high degree of self-government. Even where they work within a large bureaucracy, they exercise substantial influence over significant aspects of their own employment. Thus doctors powerfully influence the allocation of resources between different sectors of the health service; individually and collectively teachers control the examination structure and curricular content.[21] These can reasonably be ranked as strategic issues.

In one sense, therefore, the presence of professionals suggests a substantial measure of in-built employee control. But their autonomy may be gained at the expense of others, not only in different sectors of the economy or of the public services, but within the same service. The ability of professionals to demarcate and control their own field impinges, often heavily, on the quality of work and the autonomy of employees lower down the same occupational hierarchy. As C. Wright Mills observed apropos of the fragmentation of legal and academic work:

> These developments do not necessarily mean that the *top men* have less intellectual tasks to perform; they mean rather . . . that the *less* intellectual tasks are broken up and transferred down the hierarchy to semi-skilled white-collar employees, while the managerial top becomes even more intellectualized.[22]

There is something of a parallel between this process and that of incorporation and excorporation described in Chapter 5. One part of the work-force gains a degree of autonomy and influence—in this case over the division of labour—but partly at the expense of another part, i.e. those whose job satisfaction is diminished by professional self-assertion.

Professionals do not define their own area of control only in relation to other employees. Characteristically they will seek to insulate themselves against the consumer, substituting self-regulation for responsiveness to client demand or criticism. In the same way they will seek to reduce political intervention to a minimum, enlarging the field over which professional judgement holds legitimated sway. At their strongest, in short, they are protected against market forces, consumer reactions, political control, and against the rival claims of other workers. Few professions are able to achieve all these at the same time. Others groups can on occasion approximate their power in many respects; but if they are not unique they are unusually successful. How do they manage it?

Professionals draw on the same organizational strengths as other employees, exercising influence through collective bargaining as well as consultative machinery. But their power derives fundamentally from the claim to particular expertise. It is this which underpins the insistence that work must be organized in a given way. As an approach it closely parallels technological determinism. Just as the exploitation of technology places constraints—of varying degrees— on the overall organization of work and the scope for autonomy, so the exploitation of professional expertise limits other employees, who cannot be allowed to disrupt the expert. In other words, professional judgement plays the part of technology in determining, if only partially, the way many services are provided. This is particularly true of public services where a high proportion of professionally qualified workers are employed.

There is, of course, solid grounding for much of the professionals' expertise. Doctors, architects, lecturers undoubtedly have technical skills. But their authority does not derive from purely technical considerations. Again, just like technology, professional expertise is a product of social as well as technical factors, reflecting and reinforcing relationships of power.

Determining the effectiveness of a particular strategy for organizing work is difficult under any circumstances. How do we know whether health services would be cheaper or more effective if they were less under the control of doctors, or 'higher' education differently defined if university professors were more publicly accountable? But public judgement of the justification of professionals for their own influence over service provision is unusually difficult. For one of the strongest and most jealously guarded weapons in the professionals' armoury is precisely the right to decide on what counts as valid expertise. Non-professionals (be they clients, subordinates, or outsiders) are allowed to comment, but if their observations clash with the professional norm they are declared invalid. There is, in short, no authority higher than professional authority.

These remarks have used 'profession' as an unproblematic category, in the loose sense in which it is commonly employed. But it is important to recognize that occupational groups already widely accepted as professions vary greatly amongst themselves in their characteristics and specifically in their ability to assert their own expertise as described above. Examined closely, the idea of a profession appears more as a means for certain groups to achieve a degree of autonomy than an objective descriptive category.[23] Secondly, other occupational groups aspire variously to the status and power of the professions, whether or not they also desire the label as such. Trade unions, blue- and white-collar, attempt to secure for their members the most favourable conditions of service, including an organization of work which allows them to exercise their own skills (and not to be obliged to do others' tasks). But the conjunction of the professionals' insistence on self-regulation and the absence of well-defined external constraints shows up in particularly clear-cut form the pervasive problem of public-sector accountability.

The above remarks have concentrated on how far there is serious incompatibility between political and industrial democracy. A more detailed analysis of existing practices or future prospects would mean taking the services seriatim and looking at their specific occupational characters, management styles, and systems of representation. What is the rationale behind these, in each case? What is the basis for the authority of those who exercise it? How far does the nature or the service determine the structure of decision-making at different levels? How close are the links with the private sector and with direct political sources?

The argument presented here can be rapidly summarized. There is a tension between the system of political representation and the right of employees significantly to influence the formulation of public policy and the provision of public services. But the tension is not a matter of direct and uncontainable conflict. There is no necessary all-pervasive opposition between provider and consumer interests. In any case, certain categories of employee are involved in formulating policy by virtue of their rank in the occupational hierarchy, and others in shaping the content of public services by virtue of their more or less successful assertion of professional authority. And if employment relationships in the public sector are pushed further into alignment with those of the private sector, we can expect as a corollary pressures for more explicit forms of participation. At the same time all those involved—politicians, senior officials, public-service unions, and the professions—can expect a sharper public awareness of the implications, and strong pressures for new forms of accountability.

8 Worker directors—worker directions?

During the 1970s the debate on industrial democracy was dominated by the deliberations of the Bullock Committee. Its remit was narrow: to consider how an extension of industrial democracy could be achieved by means of representation on boards of directors. This specificity had two consequences: that industrial democracy was narrowly identified with board-level representation, and that in many quarters it was regarded as having suffered the same fate as the Report, which the change of government in 1979 shifted unceremoniously from pending tray to waste-paper basket. Industrial democracy cannot be identified with a single level of decision-making. However, company boards are a plausible candidate for the location of strategic power. Irrespective of legislative *pas de deux*, they should be looked at in their own right.

One reason for the association of industrial democracy with board-level representation is the board's apparent tangibility as a defined decision-making group. Moreover, there is a certain voyeuristic relish at the incongruity of shop-floor workers sitting alongside the managing director. At the time of the Bullock Report there were innumerable cartoons of plush boardrooms peopled by a motley crew dressed alternately in pin-stripes and dungarees. Some stereotypes made apposite points. Even the crude cloth-cap portrayals contained implicit reference to the split roles of worker directors, and illustrated the divergent social mores of top management and worker representatives. But they overshadowed complexities and ambiguities. Some of these were explored by the Bullock Committee but others were left untouched, both because of the Committee's specified remit and the time pressure under which it worked.

The Committee's chief recommendation, made by a majority of its members, was for single-tier boards in private companies with over 2,000 employees to be composed of equal numbers of shareholder and employee representatives, plus a smaller (and odd) number of directors drawn from neither of these groups. This was the famous $2x + y$ formula. The introduction of representation would follow a ballot of employees, at the request of the trade unions. Employee representatives would be chosen through the unions, who would form Joint Representation Committees for the purpose. The three members of the Committee drawn from the business community dissented and produced their own report, questioning the need for worker directors at all and suggesting a restricted form of one-third representation. This chapter is a review not of the proposals as such but of the more general issues surrounding board-level representation.

Origins of the move towards board-level representation

There are probably more strongly divergent views on board-level participation than on any other form of participation. It raises qualitatively different issues concerning ownership rights, and the most fundamental opposition comes from those who see it as a straightforwardly unacceptable encroachment on those rights. The other major line of attack is based on considerations of efficiency rather than proprietorship: worker directors will interfere with the proper conduct of company affairs, because of incompetence, inexperience, or bias.

Each line of argument from the representatives of capital has its rough counterpart within the labour movement. On property rights it is argued that without a more fundamental transformation of ownership, worker directors would be worse than ineffective as representatives of the interests of labour, serving only to legitimate the existing system. The counterpart of the business efficiency line is the argument that participation at this level would confuse the function of trade unions and impair their bargaining strength.

Support for board-level representation has often seemed less convinced and united behind its case than the opposition. The source of impetus which is at the same time most gradual and furthest-reaching is *ideological*. This may be relatively unarticulated in the UK, where overt ideological statements tend to be eschewed.[1] Yet there is diminishing acceptance of the sanctity of property rights, at least as they are exercised by shareholders. (There may very well be a sharp and increasing distinction in people's minds between industrial and domestic property rights.) The prospect of worker directors may arouse concern on technical grounds relating to their competence and experience, but the idea that ownership bestows such rights as to entitle the representatives of capital to exclude everyone from the board has a diminishing resonance. As the Bullock Committee stated:

It seems to us (as it did to most witnesses) that to regard the company as solely the property of shareholders is to be out of touch with the reality of the present-day company as a complex social and economic entity, subject to a variety of internal and external pressures, in which the powers of control have passed from the legal owners to professional management.[2]

Whatever the truth of the last clause, the implications of this view—that workers, by investing their labour power in an enterprise, should have rights similar to those of shareholders—are very substantial, and may in the longer term be seen as Bullock's major contribution to the debate. The view is simply incompatible with the idea of property rights which underlies company law.

Second, there are shifts in individual and corporate *planning horizons*. The 'company man' serving out a lifetime with the same employer is a *rara avis*. Nevertheless, the rules which govern employment conditions have changed. There is greater protection against instant dismissal and internal labour markets have developed strongly, habituating employees to the idea of careers within the same organization. Decisions with implications for the long-term future are of interest to a wider segment of the working population and to their representatives. On the company side, no modern corporation would admit to being without a strategic planning function. Although there may be a major disjunction between the horizons needed for effective planning of stable production and the requirements imposed by short-term financial accountancy procedures, there is at least an assumption of the need to take purposive action to shape the corporate future. On the assumption that strategic decisions are taken in the boardroom the demand for representation there can be more easily understood.

Third, there is the *concentration* of power. The process of conglomeration discussed in Chapter 1 has taken a variety of forms, and it would be wrong to assume that a single unit, sitting spiderlike at the centre of the organization, makes all the strategic decisions. In many instances the growth has taken place through merger or take-over, unaccompanied by any centralization of responsibilities. Significant negotiations may take place locally on pay, conditions, and other issues. Yet major decisions which override these or make them brutally irrelevant are reached elsewhere. The logical response may appear to be company-wide negotiations, but this approach encounters a number of obstacles: problems of inter-union co-ordination, and the reluctance of local negotiators to give up their bargaining autonomy; refusal by managements to negotiate at the strategic level; and the sheer organizational difficulties of co-ordinating policies and agreements covering many plants. The limitations of both company- and plant-level bargaining have given more prominence to a form of institutional participation which makes use of existing decision-making machinery to cover issues of company-wide concern.

Fourth, there are pressures from *overseas*. It is common knowledge that West Germany has had worker directors since 1952. They have from the outset been numerically equal to management representatives on the board in the coal and steel industries; in 1976, legislation raised their number in other industries from one-third to parity, though with a management-appointed chairman. Other countries—notably Norway and Sweden—have also statutorily introduced worker representatives to the board, without apparent disaster.[3] Yet the chief impetus from abroad does not derive from individual countries but from the prospect of EEC legislation. It is more than ten years since the first draft of a directive on worker participation emerged. Board-level representation is no longer the sole option, and its passage is no inevitable process given the success of the opposition lobby so far. It is questionable, moreover, how far British companies have really considered the implications for their own practice. But the existence of draft proposals put forward by an eminently unradical institution has further legitimized the idea of worker representation at board level.

Finally, *individuals* have simply seized opportunities. It was an accident of parliamentary procedure which gave one MP, Giles Radice, the leverage to force the setting-up of the Bullock Committee of Inquiry. Less redolent of Cleopatra's nose is the part played by Jack Jones, at that time General Secretary of the Transport and General Workers' Union, in developing the ideas and selling them to the trade union movement. Elliott has effectively chronicled the manœuvrings behind the setting-up of the Committee and the covert bargaining which they involved.[4] It is safe to say that without the efforts made by one or two strong individuals, the issue of board-level representation would never have assumed the prominence it did.

Yet this last factor illustrates the instability of trends. Individuals can disappear overnight and the momentum which they have supplied behind the initiative for worker directors vanishes with them. For all his personal authority, Jones did not bring about a whole-hearted or lasting commitment from the trade union movement to the idea of worker directors. Overt opposition to the Bullock Committee itself was expressed from both left and right wings; when the government changed and Jones retired there was no one to sustain active support for the idea. Not all of the other factors can change so rapidly, but there may not be the same confluence as occurred in the 1970s.

Board functions

Although the Bullock Committee found the structure of decision-making to be extremely complex, they were not led to any serious questioning of the actual power exercised by boards. For board-level representation to be relevant to the democratization of work, two conditions must be fulfilled: it must involve some significant shift in the pattern of decision-making, and that shift must broaden the distribution of power. There is no point in having multitudes of representatives participating in myriads of bodies if the bodies have no power and the representatives no impact.

The European debate had focused essentially on three categories: a supervisory board, a management board, and a unitary board which combines the previous two categories. The supervisory board is seen as exclusively a policy-defining body. Once it has laid down the guide-lines, implementation is up to a lower-tier management board. For some, this two-tier structure is essential, in that it allows representation without involvement (or interference, or entanglement, according to one's viewpoint) in the management function. Originally the TUC supported this split-level structure, but they have subsequently opted for a single tier, considering that a supervisory board could not supervise effectively, especially in the face of a united management board determined to frustrate it. If power is to be split between two bodies, it obeys some law of anti-participatory gravity and inevitably drains away from the one with worker representation.[5]

There is, however, evidence that real power cannot be confidently located even in a unitary board which formally has ultimate authority. Decisions tend to slip sideways, out of the participative body and into a subcommittee, or even out of the formal decision-making machinery altogether.[6] By virtue of their full-time responsibilities, management representatives will inevitably formulate the agenda, screening items and regulating the flow of information. This need not be done in any conspiratorial fashion, but rather in the interests of perceived efficiency.

The manipulation of decision-making is not a process that affects only boards where there is worker representation. A review of corporate practice in the US looked primarily for evidence on whether owner-controlled firms behave differently to those controlled internally by management. The influence of (conventional) directors was shown to be constrained by a dominant internal corps who can continue to manage according to their own lights. Potential boat-rockers are 'stabilized' by a number of factors: the widely held obligation to discuss matters within the group behind closed doors; the executive role of management, with the concomitant power of agenda-setting; the closer acquaintance of internal board members with company facts and practices; and the processes of interaction between members of a small group: 'People do not like to look foolish, and it is difficult for outsiders to pose questions of a challenging nature to knowledgeable persons without appearing superficial or incompetent.'[7] If this is true for external directors who are drawn from the same class and occupational stratum as senior management, it is more so for worker directors. A detailed report from the Department of Employment confirmed the power of inside management, though it focused more on procedural tactics such as the vetting of board papers and insistence on prior notice of intention to raise an issue.[8]

Three other dimensions of boardroom activity give some idea of its variability. First, do boards *initiate* decisions, or merely respond to proposals? 'Merely' may seem unnecessarily pejorative in that a stringent monitoring role is not unimportant as one aspect of power. But clearly if a body is to be accurately described as strategic, it must have some capacity to take the initiative. In the Department of Employment survey, well over half of the managing directors claimed that boards *generate* policy, which was the most active option offered to them. A mere 13 per cent chose the option at the other extreme, that of formal *ratification* of decisions arrived at elsewhere.[9] This endows the average boards with a fairly thrusting image, but two reservations have to be made. Managing directors will naturally be reluctant to acknowledge their boards as passive creatures (or, I suppose, reluctant to reveal them as such if they are conscious manipulators)—it is not an image which commends itself in terms of prestige and status. And there was a significant drop in the number of replies attributing a generating role to the board when the question narrowed down on to concrete issues such as the introduction of new products. This confirms the divergence referred to earlier between a general consensus on the value of participation, and the disagreements which open up once specific forms are under discussion.

Secondly, the *frequency* of meetings is significant. It could be argued that the less frequently the board meets, the greater its power must be, just as a top executive's desk is always clear of paper because he or she engages only in strategic thinking. Long-term planning is not something that is carried out daily. Nevertheless it is likely that a board which meets frequently has more influence than one that meets rarely or irregularly. The bulk (46.7 per cent) of the Department of Employment survey boards met monthly; less than a third met more frequently, and the same proportion met quarterly or more rarely, or only as needed.

The existence of *parallel bodies* can substantially affect the influence of the board as such, whether or not they are deliberately set up to do this. There is, as we argued in Chapter 2, no finite amount of 'power' to be divided in a zero-sum operation between different bodies. A subcommittee may positively increase the effectiveness of its parent by clearing its agenda of dross, allowing it to concentrate on key issues. But in other instances these 'alternative centres' encroach significantly on the powers of the original. The rationale may be explicit: 40 per cent of the Department of Employment sample of directors said that if the Bullock proposals were implemented the taking of key decisions would be whisked out of the boardroom before they could be contaminated by the arrival of worker directors.

In short:

> While the legal sovereignty of the board is not in question, the relationship between the possession of de jure authority and the exercise of de facto power is more complex. With a display of legerdemain unrivalled since the days of the Cincinnati Kid, most accounts of boards of directors assume precisely what has to be proved: namely, that authority equates with power.[10]

The report concludes, rather plaintively, that:

> the abiding impression of boards of directors left by the survey is one of extreme complexity. Though legally entrusted with sovereign authority, boards exist within a dynamic network of overt and covert power relationships, the shape of which reflects the influence of a larger number of interacting variables—structural, organisational, technological, historical and ideological. As yet, we are not in a position to examine how this interaction is structured.[11]

Evidently, then, there must be reservations as to the pre-eminence of boards as the ultimate corporate decision-makers. They assume such different roles that the stereotype referred to at the beginning of the chapter is as superficial as most stereotypes are. A board may formally have all the strategic power, and yet be neutralized by a variety of devices. It is not an entity fixedly pursuing a constitutionally determined role, but a collection of individuals with varying degrees of commitment to each other, to the company, to sectional interests, and to the board itself as an entity. There is a danger of taking too literally the organigram which depicts the board as an oblong brick neatly topping off the company's structure. Boards are nevertheless to be taken seriously as repositories of both symbolic and practical power and as arenas where powerful individuals operate.

The process of representation at board level

British experience of worker directors is very limited. The major source of evidence has been the British Steel Corporation (BSC) scheme.[12] More recent, but short-lived, was the Post Office experiment.[13] There is a survey of far smaller-scale private-sector schemes;[14] and foreign experience of variable relevance is also available.[15]

The BSC and Post Office schemes are the most substantial, and require brief description. Although there is no reason to doubt their general relevance, it should be remembered that they are both public corporations, and have particular industrial characteristics and industrial relations traditions. Moreover, the Post Office experiment lasted less than two years, giving it barely time to develop a bone structure let alone bequeath a full corpse for dissection.

In its original 1969 form, the BSC scheme was for three worker directors on each of the four group boards (not on the main board). The worker directors were part-time, continuing in their normal jobs, and appointed by the corporation's chairman from a list of nominees supplied by the unions. On appointment, they relinquished any union posts they held. The committee responsible for organizing the scheme felt

that it would be untenable for a negotiator (perhaps on his union's executive) to be simultaneously a member of a board which decided the parameters of (management) negotiating policy . . . In short, the principle of loyalty, according to the committee, was incompatible with the role of an active union representative. These considerations also prompted the committee to suggest a system of appointment based finally on management discretion, for (consistent with Morrison's principles) a worker director who was elected by, and accountable to, a shopfloor group would be anathema to the principle of management responsibility.[16]

The scheme was made permanent in 1973, and modified at the same time. Unions, both individually and jointly, were more involved in the selection process, and worker directors were no longer debarred from holding union office. They also began to sit in on a wider range of committees at different levels of the organization.

The Post Office experiment was introduced in 1978, after four years of negotiation and discussion. It took the form of representation at three levels: national (Main Board), regional, and area. Bullock's $2x + y$ formula was closely adhered to, with equal management and union representation (seven each), and an odd number of external directors (five). Moreover, worker representation on the Main Board was agreed upon by a joint union body (the Council of Post Office

Unions) of the type Bullock wished to see established generally in multi-union companies as Joint Representation Committees. There was no attempt to sever the representatives from their union links. The experiment lasted from January 1978 to December 1979; the joint union/management recommendation required by the then Conservative government for its continuation was not forthcoming and it was therefore allowed to die.

The standing of worker directors as representatives involves two closely interrelated aspects: the *legitimacy* of the scheme and of the representatives, and the extent to which they *effectively* represent their constituents' interests. Each needs to be seen as a process.

Participation will have a hard time taking root if the process by which it is introduced itself contravenes the democratic imperative.[17] For 'lower-level' participation, the workers affected by the scheme can often be directly involved in its setting up. But direct participation in the introduction of board-level representation is largely impossible. Its legitimacy depends in part on the attitudes of those who are expected to participate, and of those whose existing representative functions are affected.

The latter concerns primarily the trade unions at workplace and national level, who can be involved in a number of ways: they may have the right to nominate the directors from amongst their own officers, to put up names for managerial approval, to operate a single-channel method of election with only union members entitled to vote, and so on. Or the worker director system may operate entirely in parallel to the union system without any overlap. But where there is a significant degree of unionization, any worker director scheme is only likely to achieve legitimacy if it has at least the tacit consent of union office-holders. In the BSC and Post Office schemes, the unions were, with some reservations, behind the introduction of board-level representation. Being in the public sector they did not see themselves as confronted by quite the same ideological strain, and they were also able to mobilize some political impetus behind their own ideas. By contrast, all seven of the private-sector schemes were introduced at managerial initiative; in only two companies were the unions fully involved in making the scheme operational, with the involvement continuing into its implementation in only one of these. This largely accounted for the insignificance of these schemes.

Divergences between managerial and union viewpoints can cause the whole scheme to abort. In British Gas the unions wanted 50 per cent representation on the main board and similar involvement at regional level, but management rejected the idea of worker directors completely. In British Airways, on the other hand, management did not rule out the possibility of substantial employee representation on the main board, but general industrial relations difficulties intervened. Moreover, the trade union side can differ within itself; in the railway industry, ASLEF is opposed to the idea of worker directors, whilst the NUR and TSSA are committed to it.

Opposition is not immutable. In the BSC scheme, directors were initially hostile. Later they began to favour worker representation, though middle management remained opposed. In the Post Office, on the other hand, senior-management hostility persisted to the point of ensuring the scheme's non-continuation, whilst the union nominees became more committed to the initiative as time passed.

The legitimacy of worker directors depends also on the way the system of representation is organized. Board-level representation is not the highest form of indirect democracy. Participation in corporatist institutions at national level covers a still wider area and is based on far more extended lines of representation than worker directorships even in the most diversified and far-flung conglomerates. Indeed, the legitimacy of representatives is one of the stumbling-blocks in the path of a corporatist approach. By comparison, worker directors are usually at least drawn from within the company.[18] But since board-level participation is discussed mainly in relation to large companies, the proportion of workers who find themselves represented by someone with whom they are directly acquainted is small.

In most cases, collective bargaining is already established as the regular mode of representation. The fit between worker directors and collective bargaining is seldom tidy (which does not mean that it is unsustainable). Keeping them entirely distinct may allay union fears of encroachment on their powers, but probably forfeits any significance which the participation might have had. The attempt in the original BSC scheme to establish a clear-cut distinction between collective bargaining and board-level participation was based on the dual premise that the two roles could not be combined and that tenure of union office inevitably entailed involvement in negotiations. The consequence of the assumption was that the worker directors found themselves functioning in an organizational vacuum. Not only could they not negotiate, they had no organic link with the body from which they emerged. In any case, however, the segregation failed to resolve the problem of split loyalties. The fact that the worker directors no longer held official negotiating posts did not mean that they were able—or wanted—to discard the practices, skills, and attitudes which they had developed as union representatives.

The abandonment of the requirement was almost certainly a necessary condition for the scheme's continuation.

In the Post Office, no such attempt was made to separate the representatives from their unions, though there were restrictions on the extent to which they could report back. Indeed, one of the expected benefits to management of the experiment was a modification of union behaviour as a result of the union nominees' familiarization with management problems. But regardless of formal structures, the problem of unclear and divergent interpretations of what is and is not negotiation remains inherent. The lack of clarity may even be functional, allowing each side some latitude in following its own path.

The formal accountability of board-level representation is not determined only by its relation to collective bargaining structures, even where the relation is close. Huge and complex organizations have a diverse population, with large numbers of separate interest groups, divided by product, geography, occupation, and so on. How could a fitter from an engineering plant in the South of England adequately represent the interests of a laboratory chemist from Lanarkshire? Boards are not big enough to accommodate representatives from each definable unit or employee category.[19] In one sense this lack of particular ties is endemic in the idea of worker directors. For they, like other directors, are expected to look after the interests of all employees, and not only the group from which they are drawn, or those by whom they are elected. In the case of BSC, they have the same responsibilities as the other directors and cannot be mandated by their sponsoring union. On the other hand, the whole rationale for board-level representation depends on their ability to represent the interests of the work-force, and this entails drawing on their direct or indirect acquaintance with shop-floor feeling and priorities. It is logically dubious to acknowledge the case for worker directors and then seek to minimize the contribution they can make. Ambivalence about the role of worker directors is more subtle than whether or not they will or should maintain a bargaining posture within the board. It is embedded in what can be called the division of directoral labour. Worker directors are, on the one hand, expected to act on behalf of the company as a whole, and not as negotiators. On the other hand their particular contribution is to acquaint the board better with personnel issues and shop-floor feelings, just as the finance director is expected to speak authoritatively on financial matters. The more effective they are in discharging their specialized function, the more they are liable to be seen as negotiating.

Legitimacy is not achieved only at the outset, nor once and for all. It will need continually to be re-established, or the system of representation will fall into desuetude. It may also shift its basis: for example, initial enthusiasm of an idealistic kind may need later to be buttressed by tangible evidence of material results. For some forms of representation tradition provides a continuing momentum, as in the case of parliamentary democracy. But where there is no such tradition, or where its fabric has been holed by social or economic pressures, legitimation is a recurrent problem.

A glance abroad is useful here. Board-level representation in West Germany was instituted in the post-war period of national devastation and rebuilding. It had a particularly clear rationale and heavy political support. It benefited from the phenomenal upsurge in economic activity and the association with economic success. In other words, it grew as an integral part of a renascent German society, not as a graft upon it. Moreover, it is linked to a system of works councils which provide a solid base of visible participative activity. Elsewhere, and switching metaphors, the plant was carefully bedded down; in Norway and Sweden there were already a developed economy and a stable representative structure, and worker directors were introduced as a complement not a rival to a sophisticated collective bargaining system. Certainly there are challenges in all countries to the legitimacy of worker representation, from most of the diverse viewpoints outlined at the beginning of this chapter. But there is less of an immediate pressure on any worker director scheme to 'prove' itself in an unsympathetic environment.[20]

The problem of legitimacy clearly illustrates the paradox of democratization. For worker directors to be effective their presence must be at least tacitly accepted by fellow directors and by the managerial apparatus around the board. Yet if these feel their own effectiveness to be threatened, their co-operation is unlikely. And if worker directors are thus rendered ineffective, they will lose legitimacy in the eyes of those they represent. Yet paradoxes are not necessarily impasses, and the diversity and instability of the system do not allow them to impose themselves immovably.

Thorough evaluation of the *effectiveness* of worker directors would need a far more substantial data base and a longer time perspective than we yet have at our disposal. The Biedenkopf Commission in Germany is the only study which has been able to capitalize on substantial experience over a reasonable period of time. Batstone, reviewing the field in 1976, concluded that 'worker directors generally had little effect on anything'—good or bad. This negative verdict was repeated on the Post Office experiment, though the detailed nature of his research in this instance allowed some minor effects to emerge, such as the eliciting of more information and some slight modification of the Board's priorities.[21] The prominent position of worker directors both raises public expectations (or fears) and ensures that they are under particular constraints, especially when they are operating in public corporations and under 'experimental' conditions.

Some of these constraints were discussed in the previous section on board types. Others relate to the particular nature of the industry and will therefore be to an extent *sui generis*. Even within the Post Office Board, the two businesses exhibited different characteristics, Posts being more concerned with short-term manpower issues and Tele-communications with longer-term questions of technological innovation and capital investment. This made it difficult for the Board to function coherently, and difficult for the union nominees to get to grips with strategic issues. Then there are the crude market constraints of survival in a competitive or quasi-competitive economy. The tightness of these constraints is a matter of judgement and potential dispute, but that they exist is beyond doubt. Acknowledging these structural limitations on the worker directors' ability to influence company decision-making, we can turn to three factors which directly shape their behaviour, beginning with the issue of *information*.

There are at least four ways in which the use of information by worker directors can be crucially constrained, all with intestinal overtones: starvation, stuffing, pre-processing, and compulsory retention. Starvation refers to the withholding of information from employee representatives to the extent that they are prevented from taking part effectively in the decision-making process. Starvation may be deliberate or not; diets will anyway vary in their richness (q.v. pre-processing below). Stuffing denotes the reverse. Overloading representatives with information, in the form of massive detail and irrelevant material, nullifies participation as effectively as not providing any. Overfeeding induces inactivity. It may in fact be more effective than starvation, since it is less easy for the participant to complain about being excluded from the table.[22]

Third, and kinder on the stomach, is pre-processing. In a sense all data are processed before they are made to mean anything, and every meeting, formal or informal, depends on someone processing material beforehand. Pre-processing is necessary in some measure to avoid indigestion. Nevertheless, the nutritional content can be removed in such a way that the information, although substantial in appearance, provides little sustenance.

Finally, consideration of confidentiality can force worker directors to retain information. Acute discomfort can result, exemplified by the position of the BSC directors, privy to plans about impending redundancies but unable to pass them on to the people affected.

One reason why useful information is not sought out, or when available is not properly exploited, is lack of *training*, particularly in relation to board-level participation, because of the lack of an accumulated body of collective wisdom on which representatives can draw as they generally can do in collective bargaining. Three points can be briefly made without pre-empting the discussion in Chapter 9. First, however generous the provision,[23] it is impossible for worker directors to acquire the same competences as their fellow board members, whose full-time job it will in many cases have been to develop boardroom and strategic planning skills. This should not be over-estimated (many of the management trustees on the boards of pension funds are as lacking in technical skills as their employee counterparts). Nevertheless, there is a structural inequality in the knowledge acquired through occupational experience. Secondly, however, there is no objective body of skills which management already possesses and which training can help worker directors acquire. Significant labour representation will presumably bring with it at least the anticipation of changed norms, and therefore implies a redefinition of expertise. Thirdly, formal training can in any case play only a small part in the development of expertise. People learn far more through informal means, by observation, casual advice, and participation in a social or professional network. Thus for a union representative the learning process includes contact with members, with senior representatives, with management, and with fellow representatives. It also includes the availability of advice and support from the local or national union, or other sources.

A further constraint is *socialization*, or the way in which worker directors are 'educated' into accepting existing practices. The point has been well made by the BSC study.

Even if a worker had been appointed to the board who was likely to behave deviantly within the boardroom context, there were a number of other social processes at work, which we can label 'socialisation', which were likely to either eradicate or limit the potential for deviation. Here we are not referring only to the formal training programmes . . . but also to the process of social exchange which occurred between the worker director and other significant social actors in which behaviour was modified so as to fit expectations . . . On the one hand the directors expected their new colleagues to accept conventions of boardroom behaviour and the overall goals of the board which they took for granted. In exchange they were willing to accept the worker directors as *bona fide* members and to listen to them as people who reflected a valid and reliable shopfloor perspective.[24]

In the Post Office, representatives were less isolated and there is no evidence that they were socialized into existing practice and style.

They tried to manipulate boardroom norms, to challenge management assumptions, and to exploit their network of management contacts. They appeared less dependent upon management for information than the BSC worker directors; they were much more critical of management; and they were more likely to try to change management proposals and to take initiatives in the boardroom.[25]

Despite all this, their impact was still minimal.

All of this seems to have made board-level representation so far an insignificant factor in democratization. Few changes can be squarely attributed to the presence of worker directors; they do not appear to command great positive support amongst those they represent; and the direct political support which has generated such few initiatives as have occurred appears to have receded. Speculatively one could link this to two British characteristics: the piecemeal approach and the short-term focus. The introduction of worker directors as an isolated initiative gives them little chance of making an impact, given not only probable management hostility but also the range of institutionalized practices, such as financial accounting, which drive the decision-making process on. Such practices—notably, again, accountancy—give strategic decision-making a short-term focus which crucially limits the scope of participation. It allows the odd touch on the steering-wheel, but not a change of direction on a recontoured map. On the other hand, the journey has only just begun.

9 Dividing labour and ruling skills

In the heyday of industrial capitalism, authority was overt and derived from ownership; the boss bossed because he was the proprietor. Democratization refers in part to a move away from such property-based authoritarianism, so that decisions are made not by a single person's instant fiat but by a plurality of people over a period of time. Yet control may be integrated into the *process* of work, so that the nature of the job itself removes discretion, control, and skill from the job-holder. In Marxist terms, this is the real, as distinct from the formal, subordination of labour to capital.

The central issue is the rationale for the division of labour.[1] The ambiguity of the phrase itself contains the key. In one sense, the division of labour refers to the allocation of tasks or functions in the name of technical efficiency. But in another sense 'labour' can be interpreted in terms of people or classes, and the rationale for dividing them is the proverbial one: to rule, by facilitating their social control. Naturally, this is a falsely stark antithesis. Particular forms of work organization reflect a mixture of technical and social factors, and the task is to explain the mixture. As with other domains, the division of labour is subject to continual tension and negotiation, overt or covert and involving diverse sets of agents. Work is divided into jobs and the work-force into job-holders. Central to the way the division is effected is the notion of skill. For skill is integrally connected with control in a dual sense. Conceptually, skill cannot exist without some element of control.

We do not speak of the soldier as being skilled in obeying the command 'present arms', because he exercises no control: perfection consists in repeating exactly a sequence of action which has once been learned . . . Because control is essential for the existence of skill, it follows that there can be no skill where everything is completely predictable.[2]

Conversely, the capacity to control the content of work and the degree of skill involved is part of the wider pattern of power. From this angle skill is the *object* of control, rather than the *means* whereby it is exercised. Historically, the very notion of a skilled trade was bound up with control: over the right to perform the trade's tasks, the transferability of the skills from one place of employment to another, and the right of any time-served man to perform any part of the work of the trade. The equation of knowledge and power is clichéd and simplistic, but denotes a relationship of real significance.

Of course, skill is not a matter of knowledge alone. We use it to denote the full range of physical, intellectual, and social abilities displayed at work, stressing the way these are shaped and defined by social as well as technical considerations.[3] Both formal and informal skills are included. Formal qualifications, especially those accredited by the public education system, are a major instrument for dividing labour; the wide variation in the extent to which they correspond to the work that the qualified person actually does confirms the social derivation of the definition of skilled work.[4] But there is also a substantial degree of informality, where skills are not explicitly codified. Most importantly the discussion of skills applies not only to manual grades but to all occupations, including those conventionally defined as professions. For our purposes I distinguish between three types of skill: intrinsic, instrumental, and participative. Each has a fundamental link with control—of job, status, and organization respectively—and they are all interlinked.

Intrinsic skills are required by the content and complexity of the job itself: the demands it makes on intellectual, social, or physical abilities. Tension here revolves around the nature of the work and the scope it offers to workers, individually or collectively, to exercise their abilities. However, 'skills' are not objectively defined entities.[5] *Instrumentally* skill labels are used to divide up labour by rewarding a particular grade or pay level, justifying a career path, or asserting an occupational identity. Obviously this is connected with the intrinsic content of the work. It is, for example, easier to justify skilled status when the work is demonstrably complex and demanding. But the connection may be tenuous, and there are widespread fluctuations in the degree of correspondence between the labels and the work. Where occupational structures are changing rapidly, job descriptions and the skills they attribute to people may reflect past practice but bear only a faint resemblance to what the job-holders currently do. 'Skilled' status is in such cases far more a reflection of power than an index of occupational content. *Participative* skills enable members of an organization to function democratically. Some are specific to the formal process of decision-making. Others are identical with or overlap with the intrinsic and the instrumental. Professional planners are employed in a local authority to present reasoned arguments to elected members; these skills will also help them to participate effectively in a consultative body of employees, and their professional status further adds to the weight of their contributions. But unskilled and low-status employees may also possess or acquire the ability to represent their own and others' interests.

Intrinsic skills: technology and the labour process

Just as 'industry' conjures up Lowryesque images of factories and smoke-stacks, so 'technology' is associated with steel, plastics, and silicon—solid materials. The invisibility of microtechnology has only partly diminished this image.

Two factors combine to inhibit people from conceiving of technology as (potentially, at least) a matter of human choice and control. First, a machine embodies a rational design according to which it must function, and the evolution of new technology is seen as determined by scientific investigation. But this determinism is now under challenge. Increasingly technology is seen as consisting of more than machinery, and the authority which derives from its association with hard objects and hard knowledge is melting away. Rather it comprises systems which embody social values and institutions as well as physical tools. However fully automated an actual production system, it involves people as well as machines—hence the significance of the term 'labour process' which characterizes the recent debate. Secondly, the versatility of modern technology underlines the potential for choice, as it finds application across a range of process, engineering, and office work. Thirdly, the very scale and unpredictability of the impact of technology is provoking unease about its consequences. So technological development appears not as an objective mechanical process governed exclusively by considerations of productive efficiency, but as a matter of economic and social choice. How and why are decisions made about technology? What accounts for its variable impact? Who benefits and who loses, materially and in terms of control? Notions of productivity, efficiency, and power are seen to be closely intertwined.

New technical means of dividing labour have always been sought by employers and theorists, with efficiency and control as the twin motivating factors. The efficiency rationale was laid out by Adam Smith in the well-known passage from the *Wealth of Nations*:

This great increase in the quantity of work, which, in consequence of the division of labour, the same number of people are capable of performing, is owing to three different circumstances: first, to the increase of dexterity in every particular workman; secondly, to the savings of the time which is commonly lost in passing from one species of work to another; and lastly, to the invention of a great number of machines which facilitate and abridge labour, and enable one man to do the work of many.

In the early years of capitalism, directly repressive methods could be used to remove any threat to control. But as labour became more organized and better able to defend itself, workers' particular expertise, and their ability to assert their own way of organizing production, became a focus of attack. If this expertise could be undermined, the employer's path to greater productivity and profits would be smoother. As Andrew Ure put it in 1835:

Wherever a process requires particular dexterity and steadiness of hand, it is withdrawn as soon as possible from the cunning workman, who is prone to irregularities of many kinds, and it is placed in charge of a peculiar mechanism, so self-regulating that a child may superintend it.[6]

Such intentions were evident in the writings of the founding father of scientific management, F. W. Taylor. His approach was designed to break down the work process into its simplest components; to separate conception from execution, and remove from the shop-floor any scope for skilled behaviour; and to enable management to monopolize knowledge so that they would control every stage of production. Where Smith had stressed specialization, Taylor stressed the relocation of expertise, concentrating it in the hands of the few. Taylor's philosophy was adopted and developed by a number of disciples of varying stature, including—with reservations—Lenin.[7] Like most figures who have given their name to a school of thought, both the content and the success of Taylor's ideas are continually disputed. But the objective of establishing control by depriving the bulk of the work-force of skill, individually and collectively, was quite clear-cut.

Current interest in the relation between skill and control was sparked by Harry Braverman's book *Labor and Monopoly Capital* (1974).[8] Its chief concern was to demonstrate how deskilling takes place under monopoly capitalism. Braverman's account of and explanation for technological trends are both lopsided, but his major achievement has been to reawaken interest in the non-technical reasons which must be sought for these trends. Technological developments cannot be attributed to some immanent logic but must be explained in terms of choices derived, with varying degrees of clarity, from particular values and interests, which are themselves generated by the nature of the politico-economic system. For Braverman, the overriding or even exclusive motive was to deprive workers of control over their work by draining it of its skill content. This is not the place to review Braveman's arguments in depth, but two themes are particularly relevant: to what extent does management actively seek to deskill workers through technological change; and in so far as they attempt this, how successful have they been?

Management's aim of dividing and controlling their labour force is certainly one of the motives behind technological change, but only one. The objective may be pursued even at some cost in productive efficiency.[9] Stronger versions of the deskilling hypothesis argue that the objective is consciously pursued at the earliest stages of technological change: design work is specified so that skills will be removed from the shop-floor and control physically built in to the production system.[10] There is no doubt that such forward planning occurs. On the other hand, management may be under severe pressure to get a new product onstream or to respond to new market trends, and therefore have little time to consider the control implications. The tightness of the labour market and the external availability of skills will influence both management's choice of strategy and their ability to carry it through.

In straight economic terms the capitalist will normally have to calculate whether there is the trade-off between immediate profitability and greater control. If such a trade-off exists, he may perfectly well opt for a technology which increases production and profits but leaves job control in the hands of the employees. All such calculations depend on the time-span involved: the calculation may be that the cost is a short-term one which will be recouped later on. On the other hand, the trade-off may simply not exist. Efficiency and control may instead complement each other, as they appear to have done in the coexistence of the putting-out system with the growth of factories in the early years of industrialism.[11] In such cases, the incentive to achieve control via deskilling is weak.

Nor are commercial calculations always paramount in determining the character of technological innovation and its impact on skills. To take but one example, military ambitions have had a heavy influence, both in dominating the flow of resources devoted to research and development, and in generating—at fantastic cost—technological innovations, some of which can be taken up in industrial production.[12] Massive US Air Force support made possible the development of numerically controlled technology in the 1950s, and also determined the form of both hardware and software: 'cost was hardly a major consideration: machine tool builders were simply competing to meet performance specifications for government funded users in the aircraft industry.'[13] There is, in short, a range of dynamic factors impelling technological change, with different implications for the employer's incentive and ability to adopt a deskilling strategy.

The degree of managerial motivation to abolish skill-related job control is of general relevance to industrial democracy. On the one hand, there is hard economic advantage to be gained from a work-force able and willing to exercise initiative and discretion. Supervisory costs are reduced, and productivity potentially enhanced. Even a hard-line employer might therefore wish to encourage a measure of autonomy. On the other hand, the scope of this autonomy, and the degree to which it can be defended, raise problems of control if it goes beyond a certain limit. The dilemma for management is often that they wish to preserve the sort of shop-floor initiative which copes independently with unforeseen problems (and keeps the suggestion box full) without yielding too much control.[14] The dilemma for labour is to decide what price they may be paying for attempting to preserve their existing domains as the frontiers inexorably shift. Within both categories, different judgements will be made of the significance of the dilemma and of how it is to be handled.

The second theme concerns the extent to which management have been successful where they have pursued a deskilling strategy. Ironically, given that his chief objective is to reveal technology as the object of struggle, Braverman appears to regard the struggle as so one-sided that the employer is always able to implement his designs successfully. In fact, overt (for example strikes) and covert (for example sabotage) resistance can be fierce, prolonged, and even eventually successful.

Resistance to technological change has a long historical pedigree. Technically, the introduction of the self-acting mule should have totally changed the cotton-producing system in the 1830s. But the mule-spinners were able to retain control over the pace, organization, and remuneration of their work in spite of the machine's presence (deceiving Marx, who used them as a classic case of the subordination of labour through technology).[15] A more recent example is data processing, where already in the 1960s the division of (mental) labour was subject to increasing pressure for change. Yet it took several computer generations before the separation of intellectual and manual labour could be enforced, since the programmers did not wish to give up the function of correcting their own programmes at the machine. Moreover, programmers were regularly able to reject managerial demands by putting forward reasons grounded in specialized technical expertise.[16] Fragmentation and compartmentalization may divide the work-force and make them easier to rule, but it may also create no-go areas where management exercise little or no control over the job, in the face of specialized employee expertise.

The familiar (if often poorly understood) concept of Luddism often leads to the feeling that resistance to technological change is mainly a matter of manual workers irrationally and physically delaying progress. Yet professional groups can be equally if less overtly firm in their opposition where they feel their occupational skills to be threatened. Doctors, faced with computers providing diagnostic programmes which do not require sophisticated medical knowledge for their operation, prevent the delegation of the diagnostic function to paramedical staff, let alone to the patients.[17] Similar examples are available from other fields—though it is precisely one of the powers of the professions that they are able to impede the exposure of such events to public scrutiny.[18]

Like other groups, management's own skills can be threatened, and resistance provoked. The complex heterogeneity of conflict over the division of labour is well illustrated from a historical study of twenty-nine major American companies:

Taylor's followers encountered more opposition from the managers than from the workers. In some cases it came from the highest levels. Scientific management was often introduced in the course of a power struggle between the younger and older members of the management group or a part of a larger reform programme after the younger men had taken over . . . It is clear that plant managers generally, particularly those at lower level, viewed Taylorism with considerable apprehension and skepticism.[19]

More generally Burawoy notes how different levels of management will be preoccupied with different levels of the labour process, and also that there will be divergences of opinion and interest amongst different 'fractions of management': engineering, quality control, maintenance, and so on. He concludes: 'Therefore any change in the labor process will emerge as the result not only of the competition among firms, not only of the struggle between capital and labor, but also of struggles among the different agents of capital.'[20] The language of class struggle is made to accommodate diverse and fragmented motivations.

In short, there is significant variation in the extent to which managements are eager and able to abolish employees' autonomy and discretion by restructuring the division of labour and eliminating intrinsic skills. The resistance which they meet if they choose to adopt such a strategy is determined by a number of factors, including the position of the workers affected within the production process, the ideological and organizational resources on which they can draw, and the state of the labour market. It would be a mistake to assume that technological innovation affects only the lower levels of employee, leaving the position and skills of senior occupational groups untouched. There is, however, a further major question to be raised before we leave the issue of decision-making in relation to technology and skills. Quite simply, how far do management (or anyone else) possess the capacity rationally to plan the abolition of skill-related job control?

Rationalization should occasionally be resisted in explanation as it sometimes is on the shop-floor. The thrust of the current argument is away from determinism, stressing that the development and use of skills and technology are matters for choice. Choice entails the possibility of error. If there is a 'right' choice, whether that be defined in terms of profits, enhanced control, or some other criteria, there must be at least one 'wrong' option. If there are only degrees of rightness, there are also degrees of error. The arcane quality of technological change makes us easy prey to inflated projections which exaggerate even the potential for control, let alone the reality of it.

There are several vested interests involved in inflating the degree of control exercised. The junior manager will reassure his superior that everything—and everyone—is under control, despite appearances to the contrary. Similarly the vendor of hardware will stress the extent to which his system, after perhaps a little debugging at the outset, will eliminate the possibility of error or disruption by shop-floor employees. Union representatives will assure their members that it is they who are making the running in negotiations. At any level, the familiar motives of fear, pride, and gain will encourage people to exaggerate the control they have over things.

There are several reasons for suspecting any account of behaviour which suggests quasi-total rationality. In the first place, organizations may attempt to achieve goals which are in some measure incompatible—maximum short-term profit and steady growth, to take obvious examples. Adequate explanation of the organization's behaviour would have to recognize that actions which fit beautifully with one objective appear wholly illogical from the other point of view.[21] Secondly, people will come to different conclusions about the *way* of achieving a given objective. Deskilling may be one strategy for achieving managerial control, through the separation of planning and execution; but it is not the only one: a more subtle approach is to

preserve high skill levels on the grounds that this promotes job satisfaction and labour force quiescence. Thirdly, there will always be
straightforward errors. These may be induced from outside (for
example by the blandishments of salesmen overselling their products) or internally generated. One of Braverman's weaknesses was to
assume that the representatives of capital are omniscient, with all the
necessary information before them and equipped with perfect calcu-
lative capacity. Managers often lack information, and (like the working class) fail to perceive their 'true' interests. Salaman drily points to
the functionalist flavour of Braverman's assumption 'that managers
achieve the same level of appreciation of the necessity for these strategies as that enjoyed by the ever vigilant sociologist'.[22]

To sum up. Deskilling has certainly occurred, often brutally,
depriving workers of *de facto* control over their immediate environment. But it is neither peculiar to monopoly capitalism nor universal.
Part of the force of Braverman's case lies in the impact of his descriptions of deskilling,[23] but he romanticizes the position of the majority
of workers before the advent of monopoly capitalism and exaggerates
the degree of craft regulation exercised by labour previously. Shifts in
the distribution of skills are certainly not uniform. The debate on the
labour process is now fuelled by a burgeoning supply of empirical
studies.[24] Unsurprisingly, the more detailed the exploration the more
qualified any generalizations have to be; the essential unevenness of
the process of change is revealed, along with the rough-hewn and
multi-faceted nature of the concepts employed.

Deskilling itself is not a straightforward descriptive term. On what
basis can one decide whether or not it has taken place? How far are
subjective perceptions involved? What is the justification for label-
ling work as 'skilled'? Such questions lead us to examine the way in
which skills are defined and the label attached.

Instrumental skills: segmentation, occupationalism, and sexual division

There are powerful descriptions of numbingly boring work which
leave no room for doubt as to its unskilled character. On the other
hand there is work of such arcane complexity that it defies anyone to
challenge its skilledness. In between there is a mass of jobs whose
skills are in some measure uncertain and whose status is in some
measure open to dispute. The intrinsic dimension of skill derives
from the actual content of the work and the demands it makes on a
worker's physical or mental abilities. But skilled status depends not

solely or even mainly on the objective content of the work, but on the historical distribution of power within a single unit or enterprise, at the level of the industry or occupation as a whole, within and between capital and labour.

Instrumentally the skill label may be used in a number of ways: to reward a particular grade in the occupational hierarchy, to justify a pattern of progression between grades, or to assert a particular occupational identity—in other words to differentiate between classes of worker, for material, ideological, or other purposes. The definition of skills is far from being a direct function of the technical requirements of the job, but nor is it wholly arbitrary. It reflects social and cultural practices, including formal educational policies and the traditions of work organizations. It both affects and reflects the pattern of workplace power relationships.

State involvement in the provision of training and the validation of skills has expanded to cover new levels of qualification and all age-groups. This has been particularly manifest in the growth of bodies such as the Manpower Services Commission which exhibit a corporatist form of joint decision-making, with representation from central employer and union organizations. But our concern here is not with the central formulation of policy. Moreover, although formally agreed upon by national representatives of the corporate participants, their decisions can be explicitly rejected or otherwise fail to be implemented at enterprise level.[25]

The validation of skills is one area where labour has traditionally been able to exercise substantial influence. This applies especially to the length and content of apprenticeship training, which continues to be disputed by unions, employers, and the State. But the formal and informal recognition of skills has always been an issue of central concern to labour in its efforts to control not only recruitment but also the division of labour more generally.[26] Just as employers have their own reasons for wishing to see a certain grading system imposed, so labour will draw on tradition and other sources of power to assert its own system—the counterpart of the resistance to change discussed in the previous section. Indeed, 'many skills are actually the product of trade unionism itself, instead of vice-versa.'[27]

Clearly the most common instrumental use of skill definition is for the direct establishment of pay levels. Indeed, collective bargaining focuses more often on the implications of skill recognition for pay and status than on the intrinsic nature of the work. In spite of the strength of the craft tradition unions have regularly chosen to defend the grading system and pay levels of members in employment, asserting themselves less strenuously over the problematic issue of job content.[28] But there are other, more systemic, forces which shape the categorization of occupations and the definition of skills.

The first, and most general, is the *segmentation of the labour market*. Skill categories are developed which both reflect and reinforce the pattern of workers' transitions from one job to another. These transitions may be within a single organization, as part of the internal labour market, or between different organizations and industrial sectors as part of the external labour market. The literature on this is huge, and covers a vast range of views on the nature and number of the barriers which divide the labour market. Here we will focus on one approach which makes explicit the link between control and skills.

In *Contested Terrain* (1979), Richard Edwards sets out a typology of control systems, which he sees as having evolved in historical sequence. 'Simple' control occurs when authority is exercised by direct command. 'Technical' control is built in to the production system. These two systems of control correspond closely to the classical Marxist categories for formal and real subordination of labour. The third system is bureaucratic control, exercised through the development of formal rules to which workers adhere more or less willingly. Edwards matches these three systems up, though with reservations, to three major segments of the labour market and the corresponding bands of skill levels. Thus simple control is equated with the secondary labour market, populated by unskilled low-paid workers. Technical control characterizes the subordinate primary segment, where workers have a higher skill level (and greater job security), and bureaucratic control is most prominently featured in the independent primary segment. Here employees are highly qualified and able to exercise a relatively great degree of discretion in their work. Many of the skills associated with bureaucratic control are not ones that would be immediately thought of as occupational: loyalty, obedience, internalization of the company ethos—in short, the behaviour required is as much to do with normative factors as with immediate production considerations.

The typology, even with its qualifications, is unduly schematic, but it sheds an interesting light on the relationship between skill categorization and control, summarized as follows:

The system-of-control approach leads to a somewhat different understanding of the role of job skills, schooling, on-the-job training, experience, and other technical characteristics of labor. These characteristics are usually thought to create different types of labor (and so they do), and therefore to be the basis themselves of different treatment in the labor market. The relevance of these technical attributes, even their pre-eminence in certain cases, cannot be denied. However, the analysis presented here suggests that it is the system of control that creates the context within which experience, training, schooling, skills, and other attributes assume their importance.[29]

There are two main points here. (Both apply even if the threefold typology outlined is rejected; it does not matter if the labour market is seen as divided into two, three, or a multitude of segments.) First, because control is exercised in different ways in different segments of the labour market, the idea of what constitutes skill will also be different. In part this is for intrinsic reasons related to the nature of the work itself. But it also derives from the very varying degrees to which groups are able to assert themselves in defining the content and status of their own and others' work. Secondly, the segmentation increases over time, in that the skill gap between workers in the higher and lower segments increases progresssively over their life-times, as a consequence both of the work they do and their access to opportunities to learn. Similarly, the opportunities to exercise control over their own work are progressively more unequally distributed: for employees in the primary segment they increase over their lifetime (along with a continually rising income), whereas for blue-collar workers they remain low or even decrease (also in parallel with their earning pattern).

Control systems embodying particular categories of skill are not developed and implemented unilaterally. In the same way as there is, *pace* Braverman, potential and actual resistance to intrinsic deskilling, so labour may have its say on the instrumental dimension. Where new technology agreements exist, they generally give pride of place to the preservation of skilled status, even though the content of the jobs referred to has changed drastically. Maintenance of instrumental skills may even be the price to be paid by management for the abolition of intrinsic skills.

Within the broad patterns of segmentation, certain occupational groups are able to assert their own identity and achieve for themselves advantages within the labour market. *Occupational status* affects the allocation of skills. The historical fact of having achieved a certain status enables the group concerned to impose its own definition of skill. Thus the perceived skilledness, even of occupations where it is universally acknowledged, may depend on social convention as much as the intrinsic nature of the work, especially if this latter has changed significantly over time. Doctoring is a skilled occupation, but not many of the skills exercised in practice by general practitioners are of the sort which have earned the occupation its status. They are not only highly routine but are also more social or psychological than medical/physiological.

Indeed, the phenomenon of occupational control of skills can be most clearly observed in the case of those occupations conventionally defined as professions. As we observed in Chapter 7, most professionals enjoy an unusual degree of control over their work, including the skills involved. However, the process by which professionals exercise this control is not watertight, as their work cannot be wholly insulated from external pressures. New technology can threaten the orthodoxy. Its productive potential—the ability to perform at least some of the professionals' tasks far more rapidly than current practices—may be quite clearly demonstrable, not to be enveloped in the fog of professional mystification. The use of computers for standardized accountancy tasks is one simple example. Such potential may at the same time generate internal economic strains, as most professions are not wholly immune to pressures for greater productivity.[30] Professionals are in a strong position to assert their own skilledness, and to use it to maintain for themselves a favourable position in the division of labour, but they are not unique in this; the strength is simply relative to other occupations.

The *sexual* division of labour is the third force behind the instrumental use of skill labels. Sexual discrimination at the workplace strongly affects the control of skills. Unequal access to opportunities to acquire skills is widely recognized, with women starting from a poorer educational base and having less chance of further training. Less well appreciated is the way categories are manipulated to allocate women to lower-skilled occupations.

The occupations may be lower skilled in the intrinsic sense, with the result that women generally have less direct job control. But two specific examples will illustrate the instrumental aspect, both drawn from the lower end of the skill hierarchy. In the packaging industry, paper box and carton production are classified respectively as unskilled and semi-skilled work. In the carton industry women are working alongside men and doing very similar work; although it requires if anything less individual concentration than paper box production, where only women are employed, it is given a higher skill grading because it is not an exclusively female domain.[31]

In a scale-making firm both men and women experienced intrinsic deskilling, yet only women suffered downgrading. The men were retained on the top grade, though this was patently not justified by the technical requirements of the new job. Thus both the labour and the labour force are divided:

Technological change enables women to be restored to their 'rightful' grade. This process of legitimisation reflects both shared ideas in the community concerning the appropriate distribution of rewards, and is underwritten by the different bargaining strengths of the groups involved. Management still needs the old skills and is aware that the claims of women not to be down-graded would fall on the deaf ears of 'skilled' men, non-skilled men and also other women on lower grades.[32]

The latter case may be unusually blatant. But it illustrates the social and ideological basis of the definition of skill. It also illustrates how decisions can be taken by joint agreement as well as unilaterally, through conventional collective bargaining procedures or specific agreements on new technology. The negotiation and implementation of the agreements almost inevitably involve breaking new ground: extending employee involvement back into the earlier stages of the decision-making process (even if only to a very limited extent), and generating pressure for new forms of working relationships on the shop-floor. Labour is continuously redivided, for all the reasons out-lined above, but this is accompanied by a redivision of authority. Control functions are transformed along with productive functions.

The argument so far has been that the relationship between skill and control has two basic dimensions. Workers' control over their job depends in part on the extent to which they are able to exercise occupational skills, whether these be mental, manual, or social. The division of labour reflects technological factors which place certain constraints on the expertise that a worker is expected or allowed to deploy. However, such factors are not neutral and objective, nor do they derive from economic considerations alone. Technologies, understood as systems rather than machines, embody social as well as economic values. Prominent amongst these is an attitude towards the desirability of worker autonomy, collective or individual. This influences the choice of technology and the extent to which workers are permitted or encouraged to control their own work by the exercise of intrinsic skills.

Instrumentally, the notion of skill is used by different groups to secure for themselves positions of status and reward, and directly or indirectly to allocate others to different positions. The degree of correspondence between intrinsic and instrumental skills varies. Obviously it is easier for a group which exercises intrinsic skills also to maintain its label of skill. Conversely, employees without intrinsic skills are more vulnerable to the loss of skilled status. On the other hand, a divergence between the intrinsic and the instrumental can occur: low-skilled workers can successfully secure or maintain skilled status, or highly skilled workers can fail to have their skills recognized, materially or in status terms.

There is, however, a third major strand to the relationship between skill and control. In order to participate effectively in decision-making of any kind, workers need certain competences in addition to whatever occupational skills they may possess. Without them, formal democratic structures are hollow and lifeless, as the inequalities of initial education and experience leave some infinitely better equipped than others.

Participative skills: learning to represent

The practical problems of defining the skills needed to participate effectively, and of enabling participants to acquire them, are substantial.[33] Theoretically the issues can be laid out quite briefly. The discussion will be framed in terms of representative skills, referring to indirect forms of participation, but many of the points are equally valid for more direct forms.

First, there is no unanimity—even on the *need* for the training of representatives. The acquisition of representative skills may seem to be an unchallengeable asset. The Webbs were in no doubt about the need for fully trained and competent professionals.[34] Nevertheless there is a body of opinion which argues that the development of a skilled cadre of representatives inevitably fosters bureaucratization and divorce from the membership.[35] The more professional representatives become, the further they distance themselves from those they represent. We have already referred to the ability of professionals to impose their own interests on the general division of labour. The same argument can be extended to include the professionalization of representatives, who may use their status and knowledge to entrench their own position, without regard for public accountability or the interests of their constituents. Yet this should promote not the demagogic espousal of 'total participation', with its disdain for any form of hierarchy, but a broad conception of the types of expertise required to be an effective representative, covering communication and leadership skills as well as those needed to participate in the decision-making forum itself. However well such skills are developed, the problem of specialized access to information and expertise remains. Just as in the occupational sphere *some* division of labour will always be necessary, so some division of representative functions is inevitable. Equally inevitable are the tensions which derive from such divisions.

It is therefore inadequate to propose an undifferentiated quantitative increase in representatives' access to skills. I referred in the Introduction to Garaudy's definition of participation in terms of appropriate decision-making levels, attacking the pretence that direct participation is feasible or desirable at all levels. The corollary is that the democratization of work entails the acquisition of appropriately differentiated skills, with representatives individually and collectively assembling a range of general and specific competences. However, this takes us directly to the problem of *content*. Just as the division of occupational labour is not determined by objective technical considerations, so there is no neutral way of deciding upon the functions of representatives, and therefore of the skills they require.

Where decision-making procedures already exist, the key question is how far the expertise already embodied in them is accepted as given. Democratization entails the entry of new players on to the stage: are they to follow the old routine? Learning to represent would then take the form mainly of an initiation process, allowing participants to learn the rules of the game as it is currently practised. But it could mean that the nature of the game will itself be changed—perhaps substantially—in which case not only the new participants but the old players might also have to acquire new skills.

The most obvious example is board-level representation. Empirical evidence suggests that employee representatives are apprehensive about their own abilities to perform in the unfamiliar ambience of the boardroom, and vulnerable to the sort of socialization which undermines their representative status. The Bullock Report made a gesture towards the need for training, but never addressed itself directly to the problems of what sort of skills are required for the heavily ambiguous role of worker directors. For them to participate fully, should they become indistinguishable from other board members in their attitudes and behaviour, or should they assert their particularity and differences? If the latter, how far do their contributions complement those of existing directors, and how far do they conflict? To what canons do they have appeal, in opposition to current practices? Who defines what makes a 'good' worker director?

Yet similar problems arise at other levels and in very different organizational contexts. Tyro shop stewards, learn both formally and informally how to act as a union representative. In the main the initial training is straightforward, familiarizing them with organizational practice rather than political issues. But even here tensions can arise. Younger stewards may return from the training with new ideas about trade union representation which fit badly with current practice at their own workplace. Friction then occurs between them and senior representatives who wish to maintain the existing ways. Far more significant is the informal development of representative capacity. Here too newer stewards acquire confidence and experience, influenced especially by the attitudes and behaviour of senior representatives, as well as management and their own members.[36] At all levels within an organization, skills will be differentially valued, and the means of acquiring them disputed.

There are two further, closely connected, aspects of learning to represent which should be briefly mentioned: the source and the style. The acquisition of skills can be derived from outside professional help or from home-grown experience. The sources on which learners are to draw may be human or organizational. At one extreme is the model of formalized instruction from independent experts who guide the representatives through technical complexities. At the other is the Gramscian notion of the act of participation as itself the most potent learning influence: membership of workers councils will teach people the democratic skills required.[37]

Cutting across the degree of formality involved is the extent to which learning is conceived of as an individual or a collective exercise. Some of the foregoing discussion—and indeed previous sections of the book—may have implied that skills are acquired and exercised by individuals acting in isolation from one another. Yet a shift from decision by personal fiat to a broader-based system implies a degree of interaction and co-operation which in turn implies a degree of collaboration in the acquisition of the necessary skills, diverse though these may be. This notion of collective learning, it should be noted, does not sit easily with the style of the initial schooling which most participants will have received, which favours an individual competitive approach. The current education system imposes constraints on the prospects for workplace democracy, and an extension of the latter could mean that the practice of formal education will have to be substantially revised.[38]

Learning to represent prompts similar problems to those raised by the process of democratization generally. The unitary view is that learning to participate effectively means simply learning the existing rules of the game. Opposition to the ideology underlying such a view sometimes entails wholesale rejection of current techniques. Democratization of the workplace then requires an entirely new set of concepts—a new language, as it were, as Parkin has mooted in a more generally political context:

Becoming class conscious . . . could be likened to learning a foreign language, that is, it presents men with a working vocabulary and a new set of concepts which permit a different translation of the meaning of inequality from that encouraged by the conventional vocabulary of society.[39]

The concept of an alternative language is an attractive one, whether or not it is construed in terms of class consciousness. Yet in a strict epistemological sense it is meaningless to refer to an alternative language in a way that implies a total discontinuity with existing discourse. For how is such a language to be construed and in what context is it to be spoken? Of course there can be different languages spoken by different classes, languages which develop as a consequence of the particular experiences of the class concerned and whose terminologies reflect the conceptual frameworks appropriate for categorizing and making sense of those experiences. But how does a language come to reflect ideas and practices of which its putative speakers have little or no experience? The intermingling of conceptual and practical problems was anticipated by Orwell: 'In Newspeak it was seldom possible to follow a heretical thought further than the perception that it was heretical; beyond that the necessary words were non-existent.'

The conclusion must be that learning and democratization proceed *pari passu*. To suppose that skills are first acquired and then practised is to impose an unnatural sequence on essentially simultaneous processes. It is not only 'new' participants for whom problems of learning arise. Middle or junior managers and supervisors are consistently identified as the people most threatened by democratization, and hence most likely to reduce its chances of success. Their roles change as much as anyone's but it is perhaps more difficult for them than for most to acknowledge this. One of the acid tests of democratization may be the acknowledgement by those in power that they too have to learn new skills.

10 Collective interests: dimensions of solidarity

In the early chapters we looked at various approaches to democracy at work and concepts inherent in discussion of it. The approaches covered the *modes* of participation, concentrating more on representative modes (including collective bargaining) than direct ones; the *levels* at which it takes place, both within an organization and distinguishing between this and supra-organizational levels of the kind embodied in corporatist arrangements; its *formality*, or the extent to which the arrangements are explicitly codified and backed by some form of legal or quasi-legal constitution; and the *scope*, the range of issues covered. The principal concepts discussed were the familiar but elusive ones of power and conflict, and a simple framework was suggested for linking them to analyses of industrial relations. I argued that conflict permeates work and the process of decision-making, but also that straightforwardly dichotomous oppositions are rarely an informative way of depicting the nature of conflict. The idea of a unidirectional evolutionary movement towards greater industrial democracy was rejected, but I also suggested that the image of a cycle, depicting a circular rise and fall of participation initiatives, was too repetitive. Broad trends and specific events or personalities may combine to give a particular impetus to participation but equally may nullify or impede each other, yielding diverse rhythms of change.

In subsequent chapters, approaches and concepts were applied to a range of substantive issues, revealing something of the complex mosaic of participation. The link between ownership and control at work was discussed in relation both to the concept of economic democracy and to the question of employee participation in public services. Members of health and safety committees, worker directors, and pension fund trustees all take part in decisions governing their own working lives and those of the people they represent, but their current behaviour and the constraints or opportunities which will shape it in the future are highly variegated. The last chapter took up the proverbial link between knowledge and power, dealing with the relationship between control at work and three types of skill: those intrinsic to the job, those which are instrumentally defined as means of allocating status and reward, and those which are essential to effective representation.

It seems to me unhelpful both for our understanding and for practical purposes to propose a universal judgement on the function and practice of participation. This reservation applies as much to blanket criticisms as it does to naïve formulas for peace and prosperity. I began, moreover, by pointing out how similar or identical terms recur historically, their sense varying according to the contemporary context. This counterpoint of continuity and change is likely to persist, with no single direction to its movement. Working people are still waiting, and in some cases struggling, for industrial enfranchisement. They are, in the present economic and political climate, not well placed even to consolidate such localized control as they may have. On the other hand it would be facile to see the recrudescence of managerial power in many workplaces as the direct reassertion by capital of a secure and general dominance. The frontiers of control will continue to be under permanent negotiation.

Predictions are hazardous, even if they refer only to what issues will be significant rather than to actual outcomes. The issues I have discussed here may soon be supplanted. Even theoretical approaches fluctuate widely in their contemporary relevance, though segments of the intelligentsia will naturally seek to dig their particular gardens deeper. I want to conclude, however, by suggesting that democracy at work, whatever shape it takes, must entail at least one element: a degree of collective identity and collective definition of interests. The ability of individuals, under whatever regime, to control their own work cannot justify the label of democracy unless they also participate in some form of collective decision-making. The participation may be indirect and passive and the interests more or less vaguely defined, so that there is no very evident mass involvement. More significantly, the outcomes need not always, or even regularly, command widespread assent. But people must have some sense of identity with broader groups whose preoccupations go beyond the purely personal. For the Webbs, the key distinction in the regulation of industry was between individual and collective bargaining procedures. For others, industrial democracy is to do with broader issues and different forms of decision-making, but the integral link with collective action and orientations is generally maintained.

Atomistic, wholly individualized systems are not compatible with industrial democracy. There may indeed be positive tension between enhanced individual control at the job level, and collective control at other levels. Support for the reunification of conception and execution aims at restoring the traditional autonomy of the craft worker (or at providing the contemporary equivalent), but the implications of this for more collective forms of autonomy usually stay unexplored. However, the claim that participation must involve a degree of collective behaviour and interest definition emphatically does not imply a direct or wholesale opposition between collective and individual values. This is one of the three major 'false antinomies' identified by Branko Horvat in his ambitious attempt to define the conditions necessary for genuine self-management.[1] The antinomy is predictably peddled by those eager to undermine traditional forms of solidarity or to prevent new forms from emerging; it is also promoted by those with a mechanical, simplistic notion of how economies can be planned and organized.

A stress on the collective dimension sustains the view of participation in decision-*making* as a process rather than in decision-*taking* as an event. Participation is more about the ways in which issues are formulated and decisions implemented than about single moments of resolution. The formal political model of individual vote-casting as the basis of democracy has only limited application at the workplace, with its continually shifting boundaries of control.

Yet this poses the problem of defining collective identities and interests. Systematic cleavages in wealth, housing, and social opportunity persist. But the broad divisions of class, gender, race, and geography, although they regularly overlap and accentuate each other, cannot provide more than a partial guide to the way people in particular circumstances associate with each other and establish forms of common identity and purpose. We can debate whether or not there is a working class which acts in itself or for itself, or whether gender divisions are of the same order as, rather than subordinate to, class divisions. But there are only two sexes and a finite number of classes (a few more if we include class fractions, but the more fractions the weaker the notion of class itself). If we are to find out about, and perhaps encourage, solidarities which exist in the face of changes in the world of work we need dimensions which have a finer mesh. There are, I suggest, three dimensions over which such solidarities extend: those of occupation, community, and time.

Such a framework carries no major theoretical pretensions. But it supplements analyses based on class or any of the other broad factors mentioned above, in two ways. First, the dimensions offer either a continuous spectrum or a substantial number of points at which employees can be located, and are not restricted to dichotomies or a very limited number of categories. Secondly, they allow for the plurality of people's interests. Workers can only belong to one class at any given moment, whereas they may be members of several occupational groups at the same time, with differing strengths of identity. Similarly they are likely to see themselves as members of communities defined at several levels, and to operate with multiple time-scales in the conception of their interests.

What, then, is the occupational unit or units whose members' interests are to be in some way collectively shaped through the process of participation? Is it the immediate work group, the office or plant, the organization, or some broader but still mainly occupationally defined entity? One commonly heard argument is that participation is relevant only at lower organizational levels where it relates directly to daily working practices. The immediate work group is the essential unit of reference, and participation at other levels is irrelevant as well as impracticable. Often the argument is used by employers wishing to deflect attention from the prospect of sharing power at strategic levels. But it is true that participation will remain largely a matter of rhetoric if it does not substantially coincide with workers' perceptions of their identity and interests (even allowing for the fact that these perceptions can radically alter).

Interest and identity cannot be mechanically defined by reference to position in the formal occupational system. Nor can they be reduced to considerations of personal advancement. The question therefore is how can workers formulate a proper and unalienated concept of their own collective identity and interests. It is arguably one of the prime functions of participation to help them to do just that.

In a perfect world, genuine interests would not conflict. But even where participation has helped to achieve collective identities and definitions of collective interests it will not necessarily raise the level of overall consensus and co-operation. There is always the prospect of real friction, overt or concealed, between the processes and results of participation involving different occupational groupings. In Chapter 4 we referred to the possibility that co-operatives, benignly implementing their own democratic principles, might in so doing exclude outsiders. Or a group of skilled production workers, accustomed to controlling their own work in large measure and also to being able to exercise effective pressure on managerial decisions, may resist the submerging of their own interests into a broader collective definition. We can also pick up the theme of professionalism once more. In one sense, professionals are a prominent example of solidarity and collective behaviour, at national level through their associations and proclaimed ethos, and individually in partnerships. But as George Strauss has observed, professionalism 'legitimates efforts by such groups to protect their decision-making turf against the participative demands of non-professionals'.[2] In general, therefore, one group's solidarity may only be established at the expense of others. And, as we have already noted, individuals will often belong to more than one group, objectively as well as in their own perceptions. With significant shifts occurring in the division of labour, what kinds of occupational identity and loyalties will dominate, and how will these contribute to a reshaping of the overall distribution of power?

Such questions are particularly salient in a broader political sense. The long-standing association between industrial democracy and socialist political thought is readily understandable, for two particular reasons. First, they share the common objective of a more equitable redivision of power within labour/capital relationships. Secondly, they both reject the idea of the market as the dominant force in society, with citizens participating only as individual consumers or producers of goods and services. Instead, the direction of production and consumption should at least in part be a matter of conscious and collective decision. (This should not, as it does in some of the sloppier rhetoric, imply the exclusion of the market as a vitally useful instrument for improving the match between supply and demand.) But, as a consequence, both have also to confront the fact that there is no single working population with cohesively defined interests, other than in the most abstract sense. The dispersion of control through political or industrial democracy accentuates rather than reduces the problems of weighing up divergent interests and of forging policies and practice that are both efficient and equitable in meeting those interests. Yet it is essentially to the credit of any movement for greater democracy that it should make such problems explicit; there need be no reluctance to acknowledge them.

For workers, then, the significance of participation will vary in part according to what they see as their primary occupational group or groups with interests to be defined and promoted through the process of participative decision-making. The second dimension covers the relationship between these interests and those of the broader community in which they are embedded. Formal employment remains central to most people's lives, directly or as a spouse or child in some kind of dependent relationship to the employed person. Yet the dividing lines between employment and the rest of people's lives appear more and more porous. The overall reduction in working hours means that more time is available for family or social life on a daily basis, and longer schooling and early retirement reduce the length of the working life. Mass unemployment punches holes in assumptions made about the allocation of time to formal economic activity. Women's greater economic activity has demolished some of the divisions between domestic labour and paid employment, even if men have only begun to reciprocate by sharing domestic duties.[3] Moreover, there is a growing consciousness of the interrelationship between policies at work and other areas such as pollution or transport patterns. Workers live in environments physically affected by industrial practice; their lives are also shaped by how much time and money they spend on travelling to and from work, and how this fits in, for example, with their children's education. So the process of decision-making at work cannot be isolated from the broad range of human activities, and the definition of workers' interests cannot be isolated from those of parents, citizens, or a host of other social roles. This has always been the case in principle, recognized by initiatives such as Mondragon or Robert Owen's New Lanark which seek to treat the worker as a social being with housing, schooling, and other needs rather than as a mere source of labour power. But the existence of the interdependence is now more transparent than before. Obviously, too, it goes beyond the immediate context of a purely local community and into broader geographical settings, creating multiple and occasionally conflicting affiliations.

Such solidarities coincide only partially with occupational ones. As with the internal division of labour itself, complex inter-connections and rival loyalties compound the problems of worker participation. To take but one example: what happens if a company whose workforce is both united and effective in the degree of control it exercises is faced by a decision about new machinery which would improve production and the immediate working conditions but lead to some increase in the local level of pollution? Should the workers 'internalize' the costs, attaching to the company the total responsibility for safe-guarding the community by paying for whatever is necessary to eliminate the possible hazard? Or are they to approximate more closely to 'rational' behaviour (in conventional economic terms) by externalizing the costs (making the wider community bear them), but also don a second set of hats and pressurize the public administration to tighten up pollution control—redeeming themselves socially, as it were, from the consequences of their own occupational decisions? In a different field, might they press to adapt their working hours to fit in with local school times, or assume the responsibility for crèche provision? Looked at the other way, how far should workers seek to influence schools to equip young people with the skills which they perceive to be needed at work? In short, what sort of solidarities and what friction can we look for between the populations of workplace and community, on whatever geographical scale? Such questions are already latent in both political and industrial spheres. They can be and have been brought to the surface, even through conventional bargaining procedures. Once again, it is the asset and the liability of greater participation to bring them more to the fore, to allow their clearer formulation and to help develop better means for resolving them, in however provisional and piecemeal a fashion.

The third dimension is the temporal one. The notion of temporal solidarities may ring a little strangely, but it is not a difficult one. Much of the case for new approaches to the environment is based on the premise that the current generation has no absolute right to exploit natural resources without regard for the future, but rather an obligation to bequeath to succeeding generations an unpolluted and well-stocked planet. At the workplace the idea of temporal solidarity suggests that individuals do not have only their own presently defined interests to consider but are linked to others in ways which supplement or cut across occupational and community ties. Miners, for instance, have a reputation for occupational solidarity on an industry-wide scale, and for living in communities with an unusually high degree of social cohesiveness, largely coterminous with the occupational boundaries. Their resistance to job losses in the coal industry is based partly on awareness that working miners will lose their present jobs, partly on the impact of pit closures on whole communities; but it also derives from the obligations they perceive themselves as having towards future generations. The jobs are not theirs to sell. They are, of course, not the only workers to use this rationale, and it can be argued that their perception of what is good for future generations is misguided. But whether or not it impedes the evolution of an 'efficient' industry, and whether or not miners' sons actually want to follow their fathers down the pits, the position in principle illustrates one form of temporal solidarity which shapes the way working people seek to influence decisions.

Temporal solidarities do not refer only to links between workers of different generations. They refer more generally to the extent to which interests are defined within the same temporal perspective. Conflict can occur here as it can in the occupational and community spheres, and there is no unitary temporal framework. We saw in Chapter 6 that decisions on health and safety exemplify the trade-offs which sometimes have to be made between immediate economic performance and longer-term improvements in the work environment. We also saw in Chapter 5 that although pension arrangements are one example of an intergeneration contract, the consensual veneer of pensions decision-making covers substantive divergences of interest, some of which derive from different temporal perspective. These do not coincide neatly with labour/capital divergences: employees with pressing and immediate commitments will wish their interests to be represented differently from those who are concerned primarily that the organization should be able to meet further financial obligations far into the future.

Further specific illustration can be drawn from a rather different occupational context to that of the miners: university teaching. The idea of the university as a community has been fractured by the dramatically increased used of contract staff without security of employment. The result is a growing division between those academics who have tenure for life and those whose horizon stretches only for a few months or years. As it happens this largely coincides with age stratification, the bulk of contract workers being young and the majority of tenured staff older; but the trend has discredited the notion of an academic community as a relatively coherent autonomous body. Decisions on future policy and practice within universities have two distinct reference groups, their identities defined at least in part by their temporal perceptions.[4]

Some economists like to argue that greater participation will allow workers to consume the seed-corn of industry, oblivious to the need for future investment.[5] Labour is identified with short-term, short-sighted behaviour, management with responsible, longer-term planning. There is no empirical basis for this. In fact, British industry in particular can claim for some time to have been governed on a singularly short-term basis, with little awareness by decision-makers of the longer-term future. Investment in both physical and human capital is formed by considerations which by most standards are sadly myopic. My argument, however, is not that greater participation would strengthen a longer-term planning horizon which is necessarily good and which should be common to all. After all, as Keynes observed, in the long run we are all dead, and continual deferment of gratification may be outdated as a principle of virtue. It is rather that collective interests, with which participation is essentially concerned, are temporally differentiated in the sense that members of any organization will constitute themselves into different groups partly according to the different time-scales over which they conceive of their future prospects. The essence of responsible and democratic decision-making is a process of recurrent trade-offs between a range of temporally defined interests. Rather than shortening the overall temporal perspective, greater participation should give this process a sharper focus.

Just as there is a range of occupational solidarities, so there are various temporal solidarities which bind people together. Just as occupational units and communities may be large or small, so temporal perspectives may be long or short. They are an important, and often unrecognized, influence on people's conceptions of their interests, and on whom they identify with as they take part in the decision-making process. In an age which has developed infinitesimally precise means of measuring the passage of astronomical time, we are surprisingly insensitive to the relationship between time and the functioning of social institutions. And if the immediate objective of participation is to allow people to exercise control over the occupational parts of their life, this extends not only to the social dimension but also to the temporal: enabling people in the broadest sense to control their own time.

The obverse of solidarity is exclusion. The existence of links which tie individuals together along occupational, community, and temporal dimensions logically entails that others are denied access to the collective representation of interest. Participation cannot act as a comprehensive social glue bonding all sections of society together; we have seen how it can even accentuate polarization between core and peripheral group and exacerbate inequalities of power and reward. So is the democratization of work a mere reshuffling of the pack, with no guarantee of a better outcome? Of itself it will resolve neither technical problems of how to produce goods and service efficiently, nor moral issues to do with equitable distribution or the dignity of work. What it can do is to unmuffle issues which are otherwise smothered by the routine continuation of existing practice. It sharpens awareness of the possibility of alternatives, and fosters their development. There is a long tradition asserting the link between education and democracy, and arguing that the experience of democracy is itself a powerful form of education. As Cole put it, rejecting simplistic distinctions between means and ends:

In controlling industry, democracy will learn the hard lesson of self-control and the harder lesson of controlling its rules, and, in so doing, it will be actual rather than nominal.[6]

Perhaps the strongest rationale for worker participation is that it provides opportunities for people to learn from each other by formulating issues, and maybe even solving them, through some form of collective enterprise.

Notes

Introduction (pages 1–13)

1. In this century. Before that, the prior concern was naturally with the establishment of political rights.

2. Liberal Industrial Inquiry, *Britain's Industrial Future* (Benn, 1928), p. 148.

3. For a useful guide, especially to the former, see Peter Brannen, *Authority and Participation in Industry* (Batsford, 1983).

4. K. Coates and T. Topham, *The New Unionism* (Penguin, 1974), p. 44. The vagueness of terminology is not unique to the English language: 'Le terme d'autogestion, véritable mot-valise, recouvre tout un ensemble de pratiques, de théories et de démarches fort dissemblables entre elles.' O. Corpet, 'Autogestion', in G. Labuna (ed.), *Dictionnaire Critique du Marxisme* (Presse Universitaire de France, 1982).

5. Section 1 of the 1982 Employment Act requires large companies to publish a statement on employee involvement. This is interpreted as: the systematic provision of information to employees; consultation with employees or their representatives; financial participation, and achieving a common awareness among employees of factors affecting the company's performance.

6. Carter Goodrich, *The Frontier of Control* (Pluto, 1975).

7. Eric Batstone, *Working Order: Industrial Relations Over Two Decades* (Blackwell, 1984).

8. Hilary Wainwright and David Eliott, *The Lucas Plan: A New Trade Unionism in the Making?* (Allison & Busby, 1982). Significantly, management's reaction was to refuse it recognition as a plan, calling it no more than a rag-bag of projects. This may well be true according to the established canons of corporate planning, but the refusal was at least partly motivated by the need to reject the very idea of a 'workers' plan'.

9. Carol Pateman, *Participation and Democratic Theory* (Cambridge University Press, 1970), p. 68.

10. Ibid., p. 70.

11. Ibid., p. 70.

12. T. Wall and J. Lischeron, *Worker Participation* (McGraw Hill, 1977).

13. Colin Crouch, *Class Conflict and the Industrial Relations Crisis: Compro-

mise and Corporatism in the Policies of the British State (Heinemann, 1977) for a discussion.

14. Wall and Lischeron, op. cit., p. 42.

15. The 'democratization of luxury', on which nineteenth-century Parisian department stores prided themselves, meant only that access to finery was opened up to the bourgeoisie; few working-class consumers participated. M. Miller, *The Bon Marché* (Princeton University Press, 1981).

16. Roger Garaudy, 'Giving Enterprise a Human Face', in E. Goodman (ed.), *Non-conforming Radicals of Europe* (Acton Society, 1983), p. 162.

17. IDE, *Industrial Democracy in Europe* (Oxford University Press, 1981), p. 15.

18. T. H. Marshall, *Citizenship and Social Class* (Cambridge University Press, 1950).

19. A. Giddens, *A Contemporary Critique of Historical Materialism* (Macmillan, 1981), p. 229.

20. Bengt Abrahamsson and Anders Bröstrom, *The Rights of Labor* (Sage, 1980); U. Himmelstrand *et al.*, *Beyond Welfare Capitalism* (Heinemann, 1981).

21. G. Hodgson, *The Democratic Economy: A New Look at Planning, Markets and Power* (Penguin, 1984).

22. Sidney and Beatrice Webb, *Industrial Democracy* (Longman, 1897).

Chapter 1 (pages 14–27)

1. In China, nascent familiarity with domestic chores is reported to have helped senior management to accept 'downward participation'—their involvement in lower-level activities and decisions at the workplace.

2. For a pioneering approach to analysing this sector, see J. Gershuny, *Social Innovation and The Division of Labour* (Oxford University Press, 1983). See also Graeme Shankland, *Our Secret Economy* (Anglo-German Foundation, 1980).

3. J. Gershuny, *After Industrial Society? The Emerging Self-Service Economy* (Macmillan, 1978), p. 59.

4. J. Gershuny and I. Miles, *The New Service Economy* (Frances Pinter, 1983).

5. As we are discussing democracy, it is ironic to note that Parliament is at present one of the exceptions to this trend, with fewer women MPs elected in 1983 (23), than there were in 1945 (24).

6. See J. Wajcman, *Women in Control: Dilemmas of a Workers' Cooperative* (Open University Press, 1983), for a particular case study.

7. For a discussion of the categories used in classifying public-sector employment, see David Heald, *Public Expenditure* (Martin Robertson, 1983).

8. This chiefly refers to taking part in the affairs of trade unions, but presumably covers other bodies.

9. R. Price and G. Bain, 'Union Growth in Britain: Retrospect and Prospect', *British Journal of Industrial Relations* 21:1 (1983). Unions in other countries exhibit similar or more precipitous declines: for example, in the US only 23 per cent of the work-force is affiliated to the AFL–CIO, the number dropping from 14.9 million in 1981 to 13.7 million two years later.

10. British unions have long been run on a rickety financial basis. Even in the 1970s, average weekly subscriptions to British unions amounted to about ten minutes' pay, compared with about one hour in Europe.

11. A list of abbreviations will be found on p. viii.

12. Under the check-off system, union dues are deducted directly from the worker's wage, without the union representative having to collect them from individual members.

13. J. Hemingway, *Conflict and Democracy: Studies in Trade Union Government* (Clarendon Press, 1978). For an early American study on the same topic, see S. Lipset, M. Trow, and J. Coleman, *Union Democracy* (Free Press, 1961).

14. N. Nicholson, G. Ursell, and P. Blyton, *The Dynamics of White Collar Unionism: A Study of Local Union Participation* (Academic Press, 1981).

15. S. J. Prais. *The Evolution of Giant Firms in Britain* (Cambridge University Press, 1976), p. 62.

16. I. Knight, *Company Organization and Worker Participation* (HMSO, 1979), p. 12.

17. Eric Wigham, *The Power To Manage* (Macmillan, 1973), p. 273.

18. Christopher Hill, *The World Turned Upside Down* (Penguin, 1975), p. 62.

Chapter 2 (pages 28–38)

1. John Elliott, *Conflict or Cooperation? The Growth of Industrial Democracy* (Kogan Page, 1978).

2. E. Mandel, 'The Debate on Workers' Control', in G. Hunnius *et al.* (eds.), *Workers' Control* (Vintage Books, 1973).

3. Institute of Personnel Management, *Practical Participation and Involvement* (IPM, 1982), p. 5.

4. See Stephen Hill, *Competition and Control at Work* (Heinemann, 1982).

5. In his magisterial work on class struggle in the ancient world, de Ste Croix is insistent both that struggle is the appropriate term to describe the relation between the propertied and non-propertied classes, and that it does not signify political action or class consciousness. 'In my picture the masters conduct a permanent struggle, if sometimes an almost

effortless one, in the very act of holding down their slaves.' Geoffrey de Ste Croix, *The Class Struggle in the Ancient Greek World* (Duckworth, 1981), p. 66. In my own view, 'struggle' has too strong an overtone to be used in this way; some might say the same thing about 'conflict'.

6. J. Gooding, 'Blue-Collar Blues on the Assembly Line', *Fortune* 82 (1970).

7. Barry Wilkinson, *The Shopfloor Politics of New Technology* (Heinemann, 1983).

8. Joan Greenbaum, *In the Name of Efficiency: Management Theory and Shopfloor Practice in Data-Processing Work* (Temple University Press, 1979); J. Child, *British Management Thought* (Allen & Unwin, 1969).

9. F. Fröbel, J. Heinrich, and O. Kreye, *The New International Division of Labour* (Cambridge University Press, 1980).

10. One particular concept, much discussed in relation to participation, serves, to illustrate very well the importance of the time dimension. 'Alienation' is a term which is central to the debate on the impact of capitalism on workplace relations. But this argument, like the more general argument on the relation between capital and labour, only makes sense if there is some awareness of a time-horizon. On the one hand, an individual's apparent contentment with his or her present job, or a class's evident unwillingness to take collective action at a given moment is no safe indication of their lack of alienation. There may be valid reasons, palatable or not to the observer, why they behave in that way, yet such actions do not signal lasting commitment to the present order and may be reversed very suddenly. On the other hand, the assertion that people are acting against their own interests makes intuitive sense but becomes less plausible if it has to be regularly repeated without empirical evidence in its favour. Theories of alienation have major problems in accounting both for the intermittent nature of worker militancy and for the way in which political awareness progresses, or fails to progress, over time. See C. Sabel, *Work and Politics: The Division of Labour in Industry* (Cambridge University Press, 1982).

11. Colin Crouch, *Trade Unions: The Logic of Collective Action* (Fontana, 1982), p. 176.

12. A. Pizzorno, 'Political Exchange and Collective Identity in Industrial Conflict', in C. Crouch and A. Pizzorno (eds.), *The Resurgence of Class Conflict in Western Europe* (Macmillan, 1975), p. 284.

13. James Cronin, *Industrial Conflict in Modern Britain* (Croom Helm, 1979), pp. 25, 40.

14. It is worth noting, however, that Cronin operates with a very narrow conception of industrial conflict, equating it directly with strikes. This is no longer an adequate measure of overt (let alone latent) industrial conflict, a development associated with the growing proportion of non-

manual workers in the labour force. See W. Daniel and N. Millward, *Workplace Industrial Relations in Britain* (Heinemann, 1983), p. 292.

15. For variety of approaches, see R. Martin, *The Sociology of Power* (RKP, 1977); Michel Foucault, *Power/Knowledge* (Harvester Press, 1980); G. Therborn, *The Ideology of Power and the Power of Ideology* (Verso, 1980).

16. S. Lukes, *Power: A Radical View* (Macmillan, 1974), p. 15.

17. Ibid., p. 24.

18. Alan Fox, *Beyond Contract: Work, Power and Trust Relations* (Faber & Faber, 1974), p. 193.

19. Ibid., p. 207.

20. Anthony Giddens, 'Power, the Dialectic of Control and Class Structuration', in Anthony Giddens and Gavin Mackenzie (eds.), *Social Class and The Division of Labour* (Cambridge University Press, 1982), p. 32.

21. On occasions, the underlying inequality may even be temporarily reversed, so that the terms of a specific test of strength are weighted in favour of the agent who, in a longer-term perspective, would be called the underdog.

22. J. Minson, 'Strategies for Socialists? Foucault's Concept of Power', *Economy and Society* 9:1 (1980), p. 24.

23. See, for example, J. Obradovic, 'Participation and Work Attitudes in Yugoslavia', *Industrial Relations* 2 (1970); J. Tabb and A. Goldfarb, *Workers' Participation in Management* (Pergamon, 1970).

24. See Mike Hales, *Living Thinkwork: Where Do Labour Processes Come From* (CSE Books, 1980).

Chapter 3 (pages 39–54)

1. Sidney Pollard provides a good example from a related field:

'The demand to nationalise "the banks", meaning, throughout, the Bank of England and the joint-stock or clearing banks, is, after all, a clear-cut and definitive one in British conditions. Yet what difference lies in the objective, the understanding of reality, indeed, the reality, the motivation and the dominant ideology, between those who made those demands, say in the 1880s, in the mid-1920s, in the depths of depression and in the 1970s! It is seen, alternately, as peripheral and central, revolutionary and stabilising, simple and complex, and many other things besides. It is not the only constant term in history behind which, in a changing social context, there hides a multitude of meanings.'

Sidney Pollard, 'The Nationalisation of the Banks', in David Martin and David Rubinstein (eds.), *Ideology and The Labour Market* (Croom Helm, 1979), p. 186.

2. Groups of workers meeting to vet the quality of their own output and to suggest improvements in the production system.

3. Radicals too have been influenced by contemporary circumstances to speak of the future as progression through a series of stages, conflict-strewn but assured. Nor is this confined to vulgar Marxist accounts. As Richard Hyman observes in his foreword to Carter Goodrich's classic book on workshop power: 'In 1920 when the *Frontier of Control* was [first] published, it was still possible to believe in the uninterrupted progress of the workers' movement for rights and status in industry.' Carter Goodrich, *The Frontier of Control* (Pluto, 1975), p. xviii. Like the Webbs, Goodrich sometimes implied that there was a single spectrum along which progress could be projected, the only question being how fast the changes would occur. There is often a curious reluctance amongst those who write about democratic reform to acknowledge that where wider popular involvement occurs, it may have unpredictable consequences for both the nature of the decision-making process and the goals which were originally set for it.

4. *Report of the Committee of Inquiry on Industrial Democracy* (Bullock Report), Cmnd. 6706 (HMSO, 1977), p. 21.

5. E. Bristow, 'Profit Sharing, Socialism and Labour Unrest', in K. D. Brown (ed.), *Essays in Anti-Labour History* (Macmillan, 1974).

6. Harvie Ramsay, 'Cycles of Control', *Sociology* 11:3 (1977).

7. Phelps Brown brings them up shorter: 'If the setting up of a Works Committee was regarded as a risky concession by managers—and by many it was—the slump of 1921-2 brought such a shift in the balance of power on the shop floor that the concession could easily be withdrawn. But most Works Committees simply died of inanition.' H. Phelps Brown, *Trade Union Power* (Clarendon Press, 1983), pp. 139-40. Where they did take root in the private sector, it was not in the dominant sectors, as Cole dismissively observed: ' "Needles and fishhooks", "coir matting", "zinc and spelter", and "furniture removing" are hardly "industries" in the sense contemplated in the original Reports.' G. D. H. Cole, *Workshop Organization* (Hutchinson, 1973), p. 119.

8. A. Flanders, *The Fawley Productivity Agreements* (Faber & Faber, 1964).

9. Of course, the fact that an initiative was short-lived does not necessarily mean that it was not valuable and worthwhile. Unless it can be proved to have been diversionary, to have absorbed energies which could have been put to better use, the specific judgement may still be positive, both for the period itself and for the experience it yielded which may be valuable for the future. Even if it had costs, they may still have been outweighed by the benefits, like the case of an operation which fails to cure the patient but provides some temporary relief from pain. All evaluations live in the shadow of counterfactuals—'what would have happened if . . .'—and this is no exception.

10. Ramsay, op. cit. 489.

11. A more current example drawn from personal observation illustrates the importance of the time dimension to an understanding of the clashes of interest. The chairman of the Stock Exchange visited the Glasgow Chamber of Commerce to preach the virtues of profit-sharing. His case was based on the need to stimulate a more general awareness of business efficiency and profit-making, leading to enhanced worker commitment. His audience of Glasgow business men heard him stonily; their enquiries were mainly about where they were to find any profits in the first place before they would consider sharing them. The chairman's approach could be described as a rewriting of Allan Flanders's famous dictum that to regain power management must learn to share it: to make profits, employers must learn to share them. But the short-term focus of the individual employers made a meeting of minds difficult.

12. W. McCarthy, *The Role of Shop Stewards in British Industrial Relations* (HMSO, 1966).

13. See, for example, W. Hawes and C. Brookes, 'Change and Renewal: Joint Consultation in Industry', *Employment Gazette* 89:6 (1980); W. Daniel and N. Millward, *Workplace Industrial Relations in Britain* (Heinemann, 1983).

14. For example, under the high-trust circumstances characterized by Alan Fox in *Beyond Contract: Work, Power and Trust* (Faber & Faber, 1974).

15. A good example comes from the US, where both employers and unions have historically shown no interest in worker directors; in 1979, judging the position to be such that they had nothing to lose, Chrysler US allowed a United Auto Workers official on to their board of directors.

16. *Trade Unions and Employers' Association* (Donovan Report), Cmnd. 3623 (HMSO, 1968).

17. R. Miliband, *The State in Capitalist Society* (Weidenfeld & Nicolson, 1969).

18. See, for example, Barry Hindess, *Parliamentary Democracy and Socialist Politics* (Routledge & Kegan Paul, 1982).

19. K. Middlemas, *Politics in Industrial Society* (André Deutsch, 1979).

20. Morrison's view of a radical extension of worker participation was pungently expressed: 'This buses for the busmen and dust for the dustmen stuff is not *socialism* at all . . . it isn't a busman's idea; it's middle-class syndicalist romanticism.' *New Clarion*, 17 Sept. 1932.

21. L. Minkin, *The Labour Party Conference: A Study in the Politics of Intra-Party Democracy* (Manchester University Press, 1980).

22. See John Elliott, *Conflict or Cooperation? The Growth of Industrial Democracy* (Kogan Page, 1978), for a readable journalistic account.

23. E. Commisso, *Workers' Control Under Plan and Market: Implications for*

Yugoslav Self-Management (Yale University Press, 1979).

24. See Alec Nove, *The Economics of Feasible Socialism* (Allen & Unwin, 1983), for a broader review of this issue.

25. Though many of these have been substantially undermined by the confrontations which have occurred since the advent of the Conservative administration, most notably in the disputes, in the steel and coal industries in 1980 and 1984–5 respectively.

26. L. Panitch, *Social Democracy and Industrial Militancy* (Cambridge University Press, 1976).

27. Nationalized industries provide a quiverful of examples. British Gas, British Aerospace, British Shipbuilders, British Transport Docks Board, and British Airways have all had experience of attempting to introduce participation—some being under a statutory requirement to do so—and running into industrial relations problems. In British Shipbuilders, for instance, the strategy was to avoid imposing a single formula from above on all the different shipyards, and instead to encourage each yard to develop its own system within a broad common framework. But not only was the initiative overshadowed by economic problems, it also met substantial union opposition because of the proposed involvement of SAIMA, a managerial union not affiliated to the TUC.

28. As one of their senior spokesmen, Thomas O'Donahue of the AFL–CIO, said: 'We do not seek to be a partner in management—to be, most likely, the junior partner in success and the senior partner in failure. We do not want to blur in any way the distinction between the respective roles of management and labor in the plant.'

Chapter 4 (pages 55–75)

1. For a lucid discussion of the relation between industrial democracy and nationalization, see Jim Tomlinson, *The Unequal Struggle: British Socialism and the Capitalist Enterprise* (Methuen, 1982); see also G. Hodgson, *The Democratic Economy: A new look at planning, markets and power* (Penguin, 1984).

2. A. Berle and G. Means, *The Modern Corporation and Private Property* (Harcourt Brace, 1932).

3. Theo Nichols, *Ownership Control and Ideology* (Allen & Unwin, 1969).

4. For example, by S. Nyman and A. Silberston, 'The Ownership and Control of Industry', *Oxford Economic Papers* 30:1 (1978); see John Cubbin and Dennis Leech, 'The Effect of Shareholding Dispersion on the Degree of Control in British Companies: Theory and Measurement', *Economic Journal* 93 (1983), for a review of the various attempts to link share ownership and control.

5. 'The problem is that the shareholder *does not* "own" the assets of the company. These are invested in the company itself as a legal entity. The

shareholder "owns" a right to share in the distribution of any surplus generated by the company (which is itself decided by the management) . . . Although the managers may be (formally at least) elected by the shareholders, they are legally constrained to work in the best interests of the company, in the first instance, not the shareholders.' G. Thompson, 'The Relationship between the Financial and Industrial Sectors of the UK Economy', *Economy and Society* 6:3 (1977), 243–4. Further legal background is supplied by T. Hadden, *Company Law and Capitalism* (Weidenfeld & Nicolson, 1977).

6. J. Nehru, 'Extended Reflections of a Nationalist in Prison', in G. R. Hensman (ed.) *From Gandhi to Guevara: The Polemics of Revolt* (Allen Lane, 1969), p. 285.

7. J. Blasi, P. Mehrling, and W. F. Whyte, 'The Politics of Worker Ownership in the US', in C. Crouch and F. Heller (eds.), International Yearbook of Organizational Democracy, vol. I: *Organizational Democracy and Political Processes* (John Wiley, 1983).

8. The discussion relates predominantly to producer co-operatives. Although retail and wholesale co-operatives have figured prominently in co-operative history in the UK, they do not raise the issues of workplace democratization to the same extent.

9. Jenny Thornley, *Workers' Co-operatives: Jobs and Dreams* (Heinemann, 1981).

10. R. Oakeshott, *The Case for Workers' Co-ops* (Routledge & Kegan Paul, 1978).

11. D. Jones, 'British Producer Co-operatives', in K. Coates (ed.), *The New Worker Co-operatives* (Spokesman, 1976), p. 35.

12. Thornley, op. cit., p. 109.

13. See Tony Eccles, *Under New Management* (Pan, 1981), p. 356, chronicling the much publicized failure of the KME co-operative in the mid-1970s.

14. Even in the exemplary Mondragon co-operatives, the majority of co-operators were found to take little active part in the Assembly (their supreme governing body), to have little close contact with their superiors, and to be relatively unfamiliar with much of the available information about the enterprise. H. Thomas and C. Logan, *Mondragon: An Economic Analysis* (Allen & Unwin, 1982), p. 189.

15. In the early twentieth century, Eduard Bernstein dismissed the idea of co-operative management for anything other than small units: 'it is simply impossible that the manager should be the employee of those he manages, that he should be dependent for his position on their favour and their bad temper.'

16. Marx's interest in co-operatives extended to precisely this point, for he

acknowledged the continuing existence of 'managers' in contemporary co-operative enterprises but immediately added that they are paid by the workers, implying that the 'managers' are accountable to the workers and carry out tasks of 'co-ordination' and 'supervision' collectively and democratically allocated and specified. See Ali Rattansi, *Marx and The Division of Labour* (Macmillan, 1982), p. 178.

17. Eccles, op. cit., pp. 377–8.

18. Moral appeal is, of course, a candidate. 'Labour discipline must be based upon the feeling and the consciousness that every worker is responsible to his class, upon the consciousness that slackness and carelessness are treason to the common cause of the worker' (Bukharin).

19. Jones suggests that their socio-economic performance should be judged by six indicators: lifespan, democratic governance, growth and size, efficiency, employment provision, and income generation. These are partly defined by common criticisms: that co-operatives fail quickly, lose their democratic ideals, cannot take advantage of opportunities to expand, make sub-optimal economic decisions, have no incentive to increase their work-force, and pay low wages. Jones reviews the available evidence, distinguishing between three types of co-operative: where worker-owners are in full, majority, and minority control, exemplified respectively by Mondragon, Israeli kibbutzim, and American plywood co-operatives. His conclusions are provisional but reasonably favourable, especially for the first type. Co-operatives do not appear to be more ephemeral than conventional firms. The judgement is necessarily a relative one, but comparisons are difficult, since many firms go out of business very quickly. But co-operatives are no more inherently precarious than other small businesses, and can grow at least as fast over reasonably long periods. There is some tendency for the democratic governance to deteriorate over time, but no inexorable drift towards oligarchy. See D. Jones, 'Producer Cooperatives in Industrialized Western Economies', *British Journal of Industrial Relations* 18:2 (1980).

20. G. D. H. Cole, *The World of Labour* (Bell, 1957), p. 54.

21. For further details, see R. Meidner, *Employee Investment Funds: An Approach to Collective Capital Formation* (Allen & Unwin, 1978), and B. Öhman, 'The Debate on Wage-Earner Funds in Scandinavia', in C. Crouch and F. Heller (eds.), op. cit. For the opposition case, see H.-G. Myrdal, 'Collective Wage-Earner Funds in Sweden: A Road to Socialism and the End of Freedom of Association', *International Labour Review* 120:3 (1981).

22. See European Trade Union Institute, *Trade Unions and Collective Capital Formation* (ETUI, 1983), for a review of initiatives in Europe.

23. *Capital and Equality*, Report of a Labour party study group (Labour party, 1973).

Chapter 5 (pages 76–89)

1. For a more detailed discussion, see Tom Schuller, *Age and Capital: Employee Participation in the Management of Pension Schemes* (Gower Press, 1985).

2. It is worth noting that this provided a rare example of statutory, albeit one-off, participation, in that employers were legally obliged to consult with recognized trade unions over the decision to 'contract' in or out of the State scheme.

3. Francis Green, 'Occupational Pension Schemes and British Capitalism', *Cambridge Journal of Economics* 6 (1982).

4. See Jeff Hyman and Tom Schuller, 'Occupational Pension Schemes and Collective Bargaining', *British Journal of Industrial Relations* 22:3 (1984).

5. *Occupational Pension Schemes: The Role of Members in the Running of Schemes* (White Paper), Cmnd. 8649 (HMSO, 1976).

6. Mike Reddin, 'Occupation, welfare and social division', in C. Jones and J. Stevenson (eds.), *Yearbook of Social Policy 1980-81* (Routledge & Kegan Paul, 1982). One projected consequence is the weakening of the State system, so that the participation of unions in collective agreements strengthening occupational welfare systems has a broader and longer-term cost to the population as a whole.

7. In one sense it is true that this could be logically subsumed under the first category, i.e. the participants, by collaborating in their own favourable treatment, are weakening the overall position of their class and thus ultimately damaging their own interests, even though in the short term they gain both relatively and absolutely. But both the protractedness of the time-span and the assumptions which have to be made undermine the arguments against identifying it as a separate category.

8. See W. Brown and K. Sissons, 'Industrial Relations—The Next Decade', *Industrial Relations Journal* 14:1 (1983). Focusing more on the work process, Friedman's distinction between the managerial strategies of 'direct control' and 'responsible autonomy' echoes this theme of participation as a specifically divisive strategy. Management divides workers into those who are best controlled by direct command and those for whom different tactics are appropriate: granting them status, responsibility, and a degree of autonomy is the best way of ensuring their commitment to the organization. A. Friedman, *Industry and Labour* (Macmillan, 1977), p. 110.

9. One particularly blatant example was the early (1919) participation scheme at the Harvester Company in the US, which allowed only American citizens to be representatives, despite the substantial—in some plants, majority—presence of foreign workers. R. Ozanne, *A Century of Labor Management Relations at McCormick International*

Harvester (University of Wisconsin Press, 1967).

10. See Eric Batstone and Paul Davies, *Industrial Democracy: European Experience* (HMSO, 1976); E. Jacobs *et al.*, *The Approach to Industrial Change* (Anglo-German Foundation, 1977).

11. See James Meade, *Wage Fixing* (Allen & Unwin, 1982) ch. 9.

12. As suggested, but not convincingly argued, in P. Drucker, *The Unseen Revolution: How Pension Fund Socialism Came to the US* (Harper & Row, 1976).

13. Tom Schuller and Jeff Hyman, 'Forms of ownership and control', *Sociology* 18:1 (1984).

14. These issues received their first major legal airing when the trustees nominated by the National Union of Mineworkers to their pension fund were taken to court by the National Coal Board. The NCB's case was that the NUM trustees, in attempting to prevent the fund from investing abroad or in industries which compete with coal, were not acting in accordance with trust law, which obliges them to act in the best interests of their beneficiaries. The NCB's case was upheld, but in finding against the NUM the judge acknowledged that there is a widespread feeling that the notion of 'interests' is capable of several different interpretations, which may go beyond the narrow one of immediate and purely financial returns.

15. See Richard Minns, *Pension Funds and British Capitalism* (Heinemann, 1980).

16. Tom Schuller and Jeff Hyman, 'Union Training and Pensions Trusteeship', *Industrial Tutor* 3:8 (1983).

17. Minns, op. cit., ch. 4.

18. See Richard Whitley, 'The City and Industry', in P. Stanworth and A. Giddens (eds.) *Elites and Power in British Society* (Cambridge University Press, 1974). But see R. Pahl and J. Winkler, 'The Economic Elite: Theory and Practice', in the same volume, for a warning not to exaggerate the influence of non-executive directors sitting on several boards.

19. For the two sides of the argument, see R. Murray, 'Pension Funds and Local Authority Investments', and R. Minns, 'Pension Funds: Alternative View', both in *Capital and Class* 12 (1983).

20. In the US, all three strategies are to be found to some degree: for example, the central union federation AFL–CIO has instituted a computerized system to enable representatives to influence the activities of their funds, whether this be by criticizing non-ethical shareholding, resisting investment which destroys employment, or simply monitoring effective performance.

Chapter 6 (pages 90–102)

1. See, for example, I. Glendon and R. Booth, 'Worker participation in occupational health and safety in Britain', *International Labour Review* 121:4 (1982).

2. G. Assennato and V. Navarro, 'Workers' participation and control in Italy: the case of occupational medicine', *International Journal of Health Services* 10:2 (1980).

3. Study circles are groups of workers who meet at their place of work for discussion on a range of topics which may or may not be directly related to their employment. See O. Skard, 'Recent Legislation and the Norwegian Pattern of Adult Education', in Tom Schuller and Jacquetta Megarry (eds.), *Recurrent Education and Lifelong Learning* (Kogan Page, 1979). On the work environment reforms generally, see B. Gustavsen and G. Hunnius, *New Patterns of Work Reform: The case of Norway* (Universitetsforlaget, Oslo, 1981).

4. G. Atherley, R. Booth, and N. Kelly, 'Workers' involvement in health and safety in Britain', *International Labour Review* 111 (1975).

5. Equivalent committees were set up at this time in France. These have recently been merged with bodies set up to oversee the improvement of working conditions generally—an interesting example of a significant broadening of conception and scope.

6. R. Howells, 'Worker participation in the development of legal rights', *Industrial Law Journal* 4:2 (1974).

7. J. Williams, *Accidents and Ill-Health at Work* (Staple Press, 1960).

8. P. Beaumont, *Safety at Work and the Unions* (Croom Helm, 1983), p. 62.

9. Cited in P. Beaumont, op. cit., p. 67.

10. Paul Blumberg, *Industrial Democracy: The Sociology of Participation* (Constable, 1968), p. 123.

11. The fact that the process of research or experimentation itself affects the subject.

12. *Safety and Health at Work* (Robens Report), Cmnd. 5034 (HMSO, 1972), p. 21.

13. In the case of health and safety, the trade union movement made a major educational effort at the time of the regulations coming into effect (1978). Management representatives, especially line management, received significantly less training.

14. P. Beaumont *et al.*, *The Determinants of Effective Joint Health and Safety Committees* (Centre for Research in Industrial Democracy and Participation, Glasgow University, 1982).

15. An interesting example of the tension between professionalism and

democracy comes from within the health service itself in Yugoslavia, where attempts to extend the Yugoslav principle of self-management into public services have repeatedly run up against a persistent (male) professional bias in the membership of decision-making bodies. See Donna Parmalee, Gail Henderson, and Myron Cohen, 'Medicine under Socialism: Some Observation on Yugoslavia and China', *Social Science and Medicine* 16:15 (1982).

Chapter 7 (pages 103–16)

1. Although 'national and local government' sounds like an archetypal form of service employment, its diversity is illustrated by the two examples referred to in the first paragraph: one concerns an unskilled, part-time, highly feminized labour force, the other a white-collar male élite.

2. In other countries, by contrast, the acceptance of bargaining rights came far more slowly, so that it was only in the 1960s that it become properly established in such countries as Canada, France, and the US. See B. Hepple and P. O'Higgins, *Public Employee Trade Unionism in the UK: The Legal Framework* (Institute of Labor and Industrial Relations, Wayne State University, 1971).

3. H. Parris, *Staff Relations in the Civil Service: 50 Years of Whitleyism* (Allen & Unwin, 1973), p. 27.

4. The terms of reference of the Bullock Report are typical, dealing only with private companies. Even the broader term of the Donovan Committee did not prompt it to give substantial attention to public-sector industrial relations—indeed, local government is not even mentioned in its index.

5. One of the apostles of Swedish social democracy, Rudolf Meidner, commenting on co-determination in the public sector, noted that 'we are increasingly moving away from the market economy and gliding into a new type of society characterized by a polarisation between a socially dominated services sector and a privately dominated and large-scale enterprise type'. R. Meidner, 'The expansion of the Public Sector', in C. van Otter (ed.), *Worker Participation in the Public Sector* (Arbetslivcentrum, Stockholm, 1982), p. 45.

6. For further detail, see A. W. J. Thomson and P. Beaumont, *Public Sector Bargaining* (Saxon House, 1978); and E. Cordova, *Trade Union Rights in the Public Services: An International Overview* (Arbetslivcentrum, Stockholm, 1982).

7. N. Nicholson, G. Ursell, and P. Blyton, *The Dynamics of White-Collar Unionism: A Study of Local Union Participation* (Academic Press, 1982). See G. Bain, D. Coates, and V. Ellis, *Social Stratification and Trade Unionism* (Heinemann, 1973), for a critique of the concept of unionateness.

8. On the former see, for example, F. Parkin, *Marxism and Class Theory: A Bourgeois Critique* (Tavistock, 1979); on the latter, see D. Winchester,'Industrial Relations in the Public Sector', in George Bain (ed.), *Industrial Relations in Britain* (Blackwell, 1983).

9. John Dearlove, *The Reorganization of British Local Government* (Cambridge University Press, 1979), p. 224.

10. One example is the varying degrees of regressiveness of public expenditure on social services, which range from areas such as university education, favouring the wealthiest fifth of the population, over five times as much as the poorest fifth, to council housing, where the ratio is roughly reversed. See J. Le Grand, *The Strategy of Equality: Redistribution and The Social Services* (Allen & Unwin, 1982).

11. P. Self, *Administrative Theories and Politics* (Allen & Unwin, 1972), pp. 19–20.

12. Dearlove, op. cit., p. 195.

13. Thomson and Beaumont, op. cit., pp. 11–12.

14. See T. Wall and J. Lischeron, *Worker Participation* (McGraw Hill, 1977), p. 95—though it is revealing that the authors appear not to have considered the relationship between political and industrial democracy at all problematic.

15. Paul Willman, *Bargaining for Change: A Comparison of the UK and the USA* (University of Durham, 1983).

16. W. Daniel and N. Millward, *Workplace Industrial Relations* (Heinemann, 1983), p. 156.

17. It is worth remembering here J. S. Mill's view of participation at work as an important way of mobilizing and training people in the ways of political participation.

18. The Swedish Co-determination Act (MBL), applies to the public sector as well as to the private. It attempts to specify areas where the participation is inappropriate:

    'The restrictions in the public sector aim at safeguarding the integrity of political democracy, and are embodied in the 1976 Act on Public Employment . . . Collective agreements on joint regulation must not encompass matters falling within the sphere of political democracy (i.e. the aims, direction, quantity and quality of public services and activity), nor must they affect the way in which public authorities discharge their functions and duties.'

    R. Fahlbeck, 'The Swedish Act on the Joint Regulation of Working Life', in A. Neal (ed.), *Law and The Weaker Party* (Professional Books, Abingdon, 1981), p. 168.

19. See, for example, H. Heclo, 'The Councillor's Job', *Public Administration* 47 (1969), 191.

20. There have, however, been political moves to increase the importance

of management within the job specification of career civil servants.

21. In the early 1980s, however, there have been moves to increase central State control in the UK, such as Sir Keith Joseph's abolition of the teacher-dominated Schools Council.

22. C. Wright Mills, *White Collar* (Oxford University Press, New York, 1956), p. 141.

23. See T. Johnson, *Professions and Power* (Macmillan, 1972), for a critique of the notion of profession.

Chapter 8 (pages 117–31)

1. Especially by trade unions (other than in a historical context, for example in the phraseology of their rule-books).

2. *Report of the Committee of Inquiry on Industrial Democracy* (Bullock Report), Cmnd. 6706 (HMSO, 1977), p. 141.

3. E. Batstone and P. Davies, *Industrial Democracy: European Experience* (HMSO, 1976).

4. John Elliott, *Conflict or Cooperation? The Growth of Industrial Democracy* (Kogan Page, 1978), ch. 14.

5. The categorization of boards as supervisory, management, or unitary is not the only option (and even within this there are examples of '1½' type boards, most prominently in Denmark). Pahl and Winkler used the categories of 'non-executive', 'subsidiary', and 'cabinet'. 'Non-executive' boards include a substantial proportion of non-executive directors, who have primarily a monitoring function. 'Subsidiary' is self-explanatory (with one or more directors from the parent company sitting in), and 'cabinet' boards are made up of the heads of units of the company selected by division, product, or region. Their conclusion was that in all types management have various manipulative strategies at their disposal, and that 'boards of directors are best conceived as decision-taking institutions, that is as legitimating institutions, rather than as decision-making ones'. See R. Pahl and J. Winkler, 'The Economic Elite', in P. Stanworth and A. Giddens (eds.), *Elites and Power in British Society* (Cambridge University Press, 1974).

6. E. Batstone, 'Systems of Domination, Accommodation and Industrial Democracy', in Tom Burns, Lars Erik Karlsson, and Veljko Rus (eds.), *Work and Power* (Sage, 1979).

7. E. Herman, *Corporate Control, Corporate Power* (Cambridge University Press, 1981), p. 47.

8. C. Brookes, *Boards of Directors in British Industry*, Research Paper 7 (Department of Employment, London, 1979).

9. The other two options being deciding whether to accept decisions arrived at elsewhere, and evaluating a number of options formulated elsewhere.

10. Brookes, op. cit., p. 23.

11. Ibid., p. 76.

12. P. Brannen, E. Batstone, D. Fatchett, and P. White, *The Worker Directors* (Hutchinson, 1976).

13. E. Batstone, A. Ferner, and M. Terry, *Unions on the Board: An Experiment in Industrial Democracy* (Blackwell, 1983).

14. B. Towers, E. Chell, and D. Cox, *Worker Directors in Private Industry in Britain*, Research Paper 29 (Department of Employment, London, 1985).

15. Batstone and Davies, op. cit.

16. Brannen *et al.*, op. cit., pp. 93–4.

17. The inadequacy of unilateral fiat is nowhere clearer than in the case of middle managements ordered by senior managements to introduce and promote participation. They are in the position of wet nurses, fostering someone else's baby—except that middle managers are rarely capable of the industrial equivalent of lactation.

18. Where this is not so, for example where full-time union officials are nominated, the problem of legitimacy may be more than usually acute.

19. The problem is compounded by multi-unionism. Even within the single-industry Post Office, with an already existing forum for co-ordinating union activity, there were protracted discussions about the apportioning of available seats between the several unions. The presence of non-recognized unions, especially those representing management, can cause acute problems, as in the case of British Shipbuilders and British Aerospace.

20. The demand for parity representation at board level not only elicited a massively hostile response from employers in the UK; it may also, for very different reasons, have caused some of the internal opposition, from trade union representatives who saw such a substantial measure as inevitably shifting power away from themselves. A lower level of representation, whilst in itself obviously weaker, could have appeared more easily as complementary to existing collective bargaining processes.

21. Batstone *et al.*, op. cit., ch. 6.

22. The process has already been examined in the context of collective bargaining by the Ruskin Trade Union Research Unit, who have warned unions against equating quantity of information with usefulness. The key factor, they argue, is the extent to which it can be utilized, and the same holds true for worker directors. See M. Gold, H. Levie, and R. Moore, *The Shop Steward's Guide to The Use of Company Information* (Spokesman, 1979).

23. BSC worker directors were provided with five-week training courses, partly preparatory and partly after they had assumed office (J. Bank and

K. Jones, *Worker Directors Speak*, Gower Press, 1977); in the Post Office there appears to have been almost no training.

24. Brannen *et al.*, op. cit., p. 235.
25. Batstone *et al.*, op. cit., p. 164.

Chapter 9 (pages 132–49)

1. Much confusion has been generated by analyses which leap from a critique of fragmented labour to the implication that any division of labour is evil and/or unnecessary. Many of these derive from a reading of Marx's famous passage:

   'In communist society, where nobody has one exclusive sphere of activity but each can become accomplished in any branch he wishes, society regulates the general production and thus makes it possible for me to do one thing today and another tomorrow, to hunt in the morning, fish in the afternoon, rear cattle in the evening, criticize after dinner, just as I have a mind, without ever becoming hunter, fisherman, shepherd or critic.'

   Regardless of the need for a radical reappraisal of current forms of work organization, the notion of a total abolition of the division of labour is meaningless—and a misrepresentation of Marx's views. See Ali Rattansi, *Marx and The Division of Labour* (Macmillan, 1982).

2. Council for Science and Society, *New Technlogy: Society, Employment and Skill* (London, 1981), p. 23.

3. The range of approaches to skill simply confirms our continual emphasis on diversity. Organization theorists, for example, talk descriptively of capacity to cope with uncertainty and complexity (C. Perrow, *Organizational Analysis: A Sociological View*, Tavistock, 1970). Neo-classical economists calculate the income-yielding assets generated by investment in human capital—'general' or 'specific', according to whether they are valid across a variety of workplaces or only within a single organization or occupation (G. Becker, *Human Capital*, National Bureau of Economic Research, New York, 1964). Others stress the normative aspects of skills as the attitudes and behavioural traits which are valued by employers, such as loyalty and punctuality (S. Bowles and H. Gintis, *Schooling in Capitalist America*, Basic Books, 1976).

4. R. Dore, *The Diploma Disease: Education, Qualification and Development* (Allen & Unwin), 1976.

5. The Webbs, characteristically, thought that they were, so that craft consciousness, as a mere 'epiphenomenon' of objectively measured job requirements, would dissolve as the gap between skilled and unskilled work closed. See A. Aldridge, *Power, Authority and Restrictive Practices* (Blackwell, 1976), pp. 24–5.

6. His contemporary and soul mate, Charles Babbage, applied the principles of the division and subdivision of labour to mental as well as manual

labour, most notably to the process of computing mathematical tables. See Maxine Berg (ed.), *Technology and Toil in Nineteenth Century Britain* (CSE Books, 1979), p. 49.

7. 'The Taylor system, the last word of progress, is a combination of the refined brutality of bourgeois exploitation and a number of the greatest scientific achievements in the field of analysing mechanical motions during work . . . The Soviet Republic must at all costs adopt all that is valuable in the achievements of science and technology.'

8. Harry Braverman, *Labor and Monopoly Capital* (Monthly Review Press, 1974).

9. S. Marglin, 'What Do Bosses Do?', in Andre Gorz (ed.), *The Division of Labour* (Hassocks, 1976)

10. M. Hales, *Living Thinkwork: Where Do Labour Processes Come From?* (CSE Books, 1980).

11. Craig Littler, *The Development of The Labour Process in Capitalist Societies* (Heinemann, 1983), p. 7.

12. Mary Kaldor, *The Baroque Arsenal* (Deutsch, 1982).

13. D. Noble, 'Social Choice in Machine Design: The Case of Automatically Controlled Machine Tools', *Politics and Society* 8 (1978), p. 329.

14. See P. Cressey and J. MacInnes, *Industrial Democracy and Theories of Power and Control at the Workplace*, Discussion Paper 3, Centre for Research in Industrial Democracy and Participation (Glasgow University, 1981).

15. See W. Lazonick, 'Industrial Relations and Technical Change: The Case of the Self-Acting Mule', *Cambridge Journal of Economics* 3:3 (1979).

16. J. Greenbaum, *In the Name of Efficiency: Management Theory and Shop-floor Practise in Data-Processing Work* (Temple University Press, 1979).

17. J. Child and J. Fulk, 'Maintenance of Occupational Control: The Case of the Professions', *Sociology of Work and Occupations* 9:2 (1982).

18. M. Haug, 'Computer Technology and The Obsolescence of the Concept of Profession', in Marie Haug and Jacques Dufy (eds.), *Work and Technology* (Sage, 1977).

19. D. Nelson, 'Scientific Management, Systematic Management and Labor 1880–1915', *Business History Review* 48:4 (1974), 496. Sheer cultural antagonism also provokes divisions within management. In 1930 Captain Wilks tried to introduce the Bedaux system, a descendant of Taylorism developed later in France, into the Rover Company. He reached a deal with the union officials, yet not only was it rejected by the workers but Wilks was also sharply criticized by a fellow employer from the Engineering Employers' Federation, Mr Cole: 'Captain Wilks, to

my mind, is suffering from some rather ill-digested views with regard to Capital and Labour. He is a great admirer of Mr. Ford and American methods. His idea is that everybody should receive a high day rate and then be compelled to work as hard as possible and, if they do not, then they are to be fined.' Cited by Wayne Lewchuk, 'Fordism and British Motor Car Employers, 1896–1932', in Howard Gospel and Craig Littler (eds.), *Managerial Strategies and Industrial Relations* (Heinemann, 1983), p. 103.

20. Michael Burawoy, 'Toward a Marxist Theory of the Labor Process: Braverman and Beyond', *Politics and Society* 8:3 (1978), 284.

21. See G. Thompson, 'The Firm as a Dispersed Social Agency', *Economy and Society* 11:3 (1982).

22. G. Salaman, 'Managing the Frontiers of Control,' in A. Giddens and G. Mackenzie (eds.), *Social Class and The Division of Labour* (Cambridge University Press, 1982). Noble observes that it is very difficult to assess the economic viability of technology; evaluations are often based on data derived from self-serving information provided by each operating unit to enhance its position in the firm (Noble, op. cit. 339). Instances of inaccurately based justifications of technological changes can be found in the literature and almost certainly far more commonly on the ground, along with a host of other blunders, misjudgements, and failures of will.

23. For example, his account of the fragmentation of office work gives 'jogging' an unusually unhealthy complexion. It refers to the rapping of a stack of paper sheets on a hard surface to align them squarely, and the manual produced by the Systems and Procedures Association of America specifies the time allowed: 0.006 minutes for the first jog, 0.009 for the second, 0.004 for the third, and 0.007 for the fourth. Snipping, pinning, clipping, xeroxing, and a host of other activities are measured with similarly ludicrous precision (Braverman, op. cit., pp. 320 seq.)

24. See, for example, A. Zimbalist (ed.), *Case Studies in the Labor Process* (Monthly Review Press, 1979); C. Littler, op. cit.

25. There was, for instance, substantial resistance for some time to graduates from Government Training Centres who had not followed the traditional apprenticeship path.

26. A well-known early example of this was the struggle over dilution in World War I, with skilled workers resisting the entry of the unskilled (particularly women) into industry. By the end of the war, about a third of a million women had entered the heavy industries (13,000 of them entering Clydeside workshops during 1916 alone), and the working-class movement had been split ideologically as well as organizationally. See J. Melling, 'Employers, Industrial Welfare, and the Struggle for Workplace Control in British Industry, 1880–1920', in Gospel and Littler, op. cit.

27. H. A. Turner, *Trade Union Growth, Structure and Policy* (Allen & Unwin, 1962), p. 195.

28. Obviously this is particularly likely to be the case when recession makes the defence of employment of whatever quality a priority. Interestingly, though, Blauner observed a similar phenomenon twenty years ago, at a time which would now be considered a haven of secure employment: 'The unions have been mostly concerned with the problem of maintaining the *jobs* of their members, and therefore they have been relatively unconcerned about the *kind of work* their people do. With the realistic fears of unemployment brought about by further technological change, it seems likely that this "blind spot" in union outlook might continue for another forty years.' R. Blauner, *Alienation and Freedom: The Factory Worker and His Industry* (University of Chicago Press, 1964), p. 184.

29. Richard Edwards, *Contested Terrain* Basic Books, 1979), p. 179.

30. The professions, indeed, are caught in something of a dilemma. On the one hand they need to demonstrate the advanced *technical* nature of their skills, and on the other to protect the exclusiveness of their knowledge by insisting on its private or *indeterminate* quality. For an outline of this interesting distinction, see H. Jamous and B. Peloille, 'Professions or Self-Perpetuating Systems? Changes in the French University Hospital System', in J. Jackson (ed.), *Professions and Professionalization* (Cambridge University Press, 1977).

31. J. Craig, J. Rubery, R. Tarling, and F. Wilkinson, *Abolition and After: The Paper Box Wages Council*, Research Paper 12 (Department of Employment, London, 1980).

32. T. Mainwaring, *The Extended Internal Labour Market*, 11M-LMP 82-29 (International Institute of Management, Berlin, 1982), p. 54.

33. T. Schuller, 'The Democratization of Work: Educational Implications', in Tom Schuller and Jacquetta Megarry (eds.), *Recurrent Education and Lifelong Learning* (Kogan Page, 1979).

34. Sidney and Beatrice Webb, *Industrial Democracy* (Longman, 1897), p. 204.

35. See, for example, Richard Hyman, 'The Politics of Workplace Trade Unionism', *Capital and Class* 9 (1979).

36. See Don Robertson and Tom Schuller, *Stewards, Members, and Trade Union Training*, Centre for Research in Industrial Democracy and Participation Discussion Paper 6 (Glasgow University, 1982).

37. See Leszek Kolakowski, *Main Currents of Marxism*, vol. III: *The Breakdown* (Clarendon Press, 1978), p. 231.

38. See H. Levin, 'Education and Organizational Democracy', in C. Crouch and F. Heller (eds.), *International Yearbook of Organizational Democracy*,

vol. I; *Organizational Democracy and Political Processes* (John Wiley, 1983).

39. F. Parkin, *Class Inequality and Political Order* (Paladin, 1972), p. 90.

Chapter 10 (pages 150–8)

1. Branko Horvat, *The Political Economy of Socialism* (Martin Robertson, 1982).

2. George Strauss, 'Workers' Participation in Management: An International Perspective', *Research in Organizational Behavior* 4 (1982), 237.

3. See R. E. Pahl, *Divisions of Labour* (Blackwell, 1984).

4. Individual academics will, of course, retain disciplinary and other loyalties.

5. Compare Macaulay's early-nineteenth-century prophecy that the consequences of universal adult suffrage would be the destruction of civilized society through the use of its capital stock for current consumption (see John Dunn, *The Politics of Socialism: An Essay in Political Theory*, Cambridge University Press, 1984, p. 19).

6. G. D. H. Cole, *The World of Labour* (Bell, 1917), p. 28.

Further reading

Abrahamsson, Bengt, *Bureaucracy or Participation* (Sage, 1977).

Bank, J., and Jones, K., *Worker-Directors Speak* (Gower Press, 1977).

Batstone, Eric, *Working Order: Industrial Relations over Two Decades* (Blackwell, 1984).

——, and Davies, P., *Industrial Democracy: European Experience* (HMSO, 1976).

——, Ferner, A., and Terry, M., *Unions on the Board: An Experiment in Industrial Democracy* (Blackwell, 1983).

Berle, A., and Means, G., *The Modern Corporation and Private Property* (Harcourt Brace, 1932).

Blauner, Robert, *Alienation and Freedom: The Factory Worker and His Industry* (University of Chicago Press, 1964).

Blumberg, Paul, *Industrial Democracy: The Sociology of Participation* (Constable, 1968).

Brannen, Peter, *Authority and Participation in Industry* (Batsford, 1983).

——, Batstone, E., Fatchett, D., and White, P., *The Worker Directors* (Hutchinson, 1976).

Braverman, Harry, *Labor and Monopoly Capital* (Monthly Review Press, 1974).

Brookes, Christopher, *Boards of Directors in British Industry*, Research Paper No. 7 (Department of Employment, London, 1979).

Bullock Report, *Report of the Committee of Inquiry on Industrial Democracy*, Cmnd. 6706 (HMSO, 1977).

Burns, Tom R., Karlsson, Lars Erik, and Rus, Veljko, *Work and Power: The Liberation of Work and the Control of Political Power* (Sage, 1979).

Clegg, H. A., *A New Approach to Industrial Democracy* (Blackwell, 1960).

——, *The Changing System of Industrial Relations in Great Britain* (Blackwell, 1980).

Coates, Ken, *The New Worker Cooperatives* (Spokesman Books, 1976).

Cole, G. D. H., *Self-Government in Industry* (Hutchinson, 1972).

——, *Workshop Organization* (Hutchinson, 1973).

Commisso, E. T., *Workers Control under Plan and Market: Implications for Yugoslav Self-Management* (Yale University Press, 1973).

Cressey, P., Eldridge, J., MacInnes, J., and Norris, G., *Industrial Democracy and Participation: A Scottish Survey*, Research Paper No. 28 (Department of Employment, London, 1981).

Crouch, C., and Heller, F. A. (eds.), *International Yearbook of Organizational Democracy*, vol. I: *Organizational Democracy and Political Processes* (John Wiley, 1983).

Daniel, W., and Millward, N., *Workplace Industrial Relations* (Heinemann, 1983).

Donovan Report, *Trade Unions and Employers' Associations: Report*, Cmnd. 3623 (HMSO, 1968).

Dowling, M. J., Goodman, F. B., Gotting, D. A., and Hyman, J. D., *Employee Participation: Practice and Attitudes in North West Manufacturing Industry*, Research Paper No. 27 (Department of Employment, London, 1981).

Eccles, Tony, *Under New Management* (Pan, 1981).

Elliot, John, *Conflict or Cooperation? The Growth of Industrial Democracy* (Kogan Page, 1978).

Emery, Fred, and Thorsrud, Einar, *Democracy at Work* (Martinus Nijhoff, 1976).

Espinosa, Juan G., and Zimbalist, Andrew S., *Economic Democracy. Workers Participation in Chilean Industry, 1970–73* (Academic Press, 1978).

Fox, A., *Beyond Contract: Work, Power and Trust Relations* (Faber & Faber, 1974).

Friedman. A., *Industry and Labour* (Macmillan, 1977).

Garson, David, *Workers' Self-Management in Industry—The West European Experience* (Praeger, 1977).

Goodrich, Carter, *The Frontier of Control* (Pluto, 1975).

Gospel, H. and Littler, C. (eds.), *Managerial Strategies and Industrial Relations* (Heinemann, 1983).

Gustavsen, Bjorn, and Hunnius, Gerry, *New Patterns of Work Reform: The Case of Norway* (Oslo, Universitetsforlaget, 1981).

Herman, E., *Corporate Control, Corporate Power* (Cambridge University Press, 1981).

Hill, Stephen, *Competition and Control at Work* (Heinemann, 1982).

Hodgson, Geoff, *The Democratic Economy* (Penguin, 1984).

Horvat, Branko, *The Political Economy of Socialism* (Martin Robertson, 1982).

Hunnius, Gerry, Garson, G. D., and Case, J. (eds.), *Workers' Control* (Vintage Books, 1973).

IDE, *Industrial Democracy in Europe* (Oxford University Press, 1982).

IPM, *Practical Participation and Involvement* (Institute of Personnel Management, London, 1982).

Knight, I., *Company Organization and Worker Participation* (HMSO, 1979).

Kolaja, J., *Workers' Councils: The Yugoslav Experiment* (Tavistock, 1965).

Littler, C., *The Development of the Labour Process in Capitalist Societies* (Heinemann, 1983).

Marchington, Mick, *Responses to Participation at Work* (Gower, 1980).

Marsden, David, *Industrial Democracy and Industrial Control in West Germany, France and Great Britain* Research Paper No. 4 (Department of Employment, London, 1978).

Meidner, R., *Employee Investment Funds: An Approach to Collective Capital Formation* (Allen & Unwin, 1978).

Nicholson, N., Ursell, G., and Blyton, P., *The Dynamics of White Collar Unionism: A study of Local Union Participation* (Academic Press, London, 1981).

Parris, H., *Staff Relations in the Civil Service—50 Years of Whitleyism* (Allen & Unwin, 1973).

Pateman, Carole, *Participation and Democratic Theory* (Cambridge University Press, 1970).

Phelps Brown, H., *Trade Union Power* (Clarendon Press, 1983).

Poole, Michael, *Workers' Participation in Industry* (Routledge and Kegan Paul, 1978).

Pribicevic, B., *Shop Stewards' Movement and Workers' Control* (Blackwell, 1959).

Radice, Giles *The Industrial Democrats: Trade Unions in a Changing World* (Allen & Unwin, 1982).

Sabel, C., *Work and Politics: The Division of Labour in Industry* (Cambridge University Press, 1982).

Thomas, H. and Logan, C., *Mondragon: An Economic Analysis* (Allen & Unwin, 1982).

Thornley, J., *Workers' Cooperatives: Jobs and Dreams* (Heinemann, 1981).

Tomlinson J., *The Unequal Struggle: British Socialism and the Capitalist Enterprise* (Methuen, 1982).

Towers, B., Chell, E., and Cox, D., *Worker Directors in Private Industry*, Research Paper No. 29 (Department of Employment, London, 1985).

Vanek, Jaroslav, *Self-Management: Economic Liberation of Man* (Penguin, 1957).

van Otter, Casten (ed.), *Worker Participation in the Public Sector* (Arbetslivcentrum, Stockholm, 1982).

Wajcman, J., *Woman in Control: Dilemmas of a Workers' Cooperative* (Open University Press, 1983).

Wall, T., and Lischeron, J., *Worker Participation* (McGraw Hill, 1977).

Webb, S. and B., *Industrial Democracy* (Longman, 1987).

Index